GEMS

From God's Treasury

Rosie Soroka M.S.

Order this book online at www.trafford.com
or email orders@trafford.com

Most Trafford titles are also available at major online book retailers.

Printed in the United States of America.

ISBN: 978-1-4269-7537-0 (sc)
ISBN: 978-1-4269-7538-7 (e)

Trafford rev. 09/21/2011

 www.trafford.com

North America & international
toll-free: 1 888 232 4444 (USA & Canada)
phone: 250 383 6864 ✦ fax: 812 355 4082

Contents

Part II: Prayers   **123**

Part III: Psalms   **145**

This book is so dedicated to the Love of my life. You have restored my heart and saved my soul, You have captivated me and I am no longer my own. I Love you Jesus.

Features:

This book includes scriptures with easy to follow examples and how they apply in daily life. At the end of these examples is included a suggested exercise to really put that verse in motion in your life and some even have additional prayers.

The next section in the book includes various prayers that unleash supernatural blessings. These prayers will teach you how to use the Word of God in your prayer and at the same time allow you the flexibility to add your own petitions.

Lastly, the last portion of the book includes Psalms that I have written. Although these Psalms are very personal, God wanted me to include them in this book, so there they are. However I encourage you to write your own psalms and continue to build an intimate relationship with Him on your own.

PART I
TREASURED REVELATIONS

~A Special Note:~

Many times in a journey different paths are set before us to decide which one to take. The truth is that there only lies one path that is the correct one. Not everyone is meant to be an Apostle or a Pastor, however everyone is called to God and according to your measure of faith your purpose is established. Life began for all struggling to take that first breath of air, for some you were planned and for others it is a miracle that you are here. The point is that you are here, and you, yes you have a plan and purpose here on Earth. If you so choice to accept it you will be surrounded by adventures, life, power, anointing, grace, favor, and a special stamp on your soul given to you by the Holy Spirit. I so pray that you do accept your calling, you will not regret it. God is an extravagant God and He displays His love for His children in extravagant ways and He rewards His children with extravagant gifts.

~ENDURANCE~

Matthew 10:22
".....but he that *endureth* to the end shall be saved."

The definition of Endure is the following:
1. *Bear* hardship: to experience exertion, pain, or hardship without giving up
2. *Tolerate* disagreeable things: to tolerate or accept somebody or something that is extremely disagreeable
3. *Survive*: to last or survive over a period of time, especially when faced with difficulties

One of the devil's jobs is to wear out the saints by throwing in their way obstacles. Jesus knew this and this is why He didn't say we need to *stay this way* until the end, He said **"endureth to the end.."** So today look at your situation and know that God is with you and knows your intentions and heart. He also knows that you need things to endure whether its love, patience, healing, health, forgiveness, or anything else just ask Him in faith and He will give it to you. Keep fighting the Good Fight.

My Prayer For You:

God almighty, I put myself in the front lines to pray for you children today Lord, I pray that Your hand is over them guiding them and showing them Your ways. I pray in the name of Jesus that You give Your children an unbearable hunger for Your Word so that they may endure knowing the difference between right and wrong, Your promises and the lies of the devil. Father I pray that as Your children study Your Word that their swords become sharper and sharper and they become stronger and stronger. Lord give us all what we need in this day to fight the Good Fight in Your name and to endure in Christ until our last breath. (Now you say the things that you need out loud).... Father in this day I need......
in Jesus name. Amen.

~Renewal~

Romans 12:2 : Do not be conformed to this world (this age), [fashioned after and adapted to its external, superficial customs], but be transformed (changed) by the [entire] renewal of your mind [by its new ideals and its new attitude], so that you may prove [for yourselves] what is the good and acceptable and perfect will of God, even the thing which is good and acceptable and perfect [in His sight for you].

Ephesians 4:23 : And be constantly renewed in the spirit of your mind (having a fresh mental and spiritual attitude)

Can you imagine trying to download 2,000 songs to a computer built in 1980? It's funny to think about things that are obsolete. Growing up I remember the phones used were the sizes of bricks, literally, they were big and only served two functions; to make very expensive calls or to beat down a mugger.

Did you know people can also become obsolete? Would you go to a doctor that graduated in 1976 and never took up any additional training's, or never even read another article about human health? Probably not. Christians can also suffer from what I call 'obsoletism.' These people usually stink spiritually because they do a lot of walking in the flesh (criticize, gossip, etc.). These people usually depend on others to fill them up or depend on religious actions and rituals to get what they think is a "relationship with God" then complain about it.

However a Christian who has renewed their minds are the exact opposite and walk in love, patience, compassion for others, and excrete spiritual fragrance at Gods feet. And let me tell you when God inhales that fragrance given off by a renewed Christian...miracles happen, the 'all of a suddens' start happening, and things begin to change. You begin to move from glory to glory and from victory to victory.

Some may wonder and ask well how do I get renewed? Well that depends on where you are on your walk with our Daddy. If you are just starting out a good place to begin is by playing some good worship music, praying, going to a church that God has lead you to, and reading the Bible. It may sound somewhat boring at first, but as your intimacy with God grows the more adventurous your life will get, I guarantee it.

Today I challenge you to renew your minds in prayer and in intimate communion with God and transform your walk to transform the world.

~Woman~

Genesis 3:20: The man called his wife's name Eve [life spring], because she was the mother of all the living.

Ever wonder why women all over the world and throughout time have been so greatly discriminated against? Even today in modern age and yes in the United States women continue to be discriminated against, this is evident in what the news calls the glass ceiling effect: "The term 'glass ceiling' refers to gender discrimination that limits a woman as inferior and is harassed by the society." In other parts of the world if a woman shows her face she is stoned to death and yet still in other parts of the world little girls are being circumcised.

Whether you are single woman, recently divorced, a single mother, a daughter, a wife, or whatever else; I bet it has been challenging.

You see you are on the enemies' hit list from the moment you crash-landed on your head here. You can do amazing things that he only wishes he could do, you can create new things and not just copy what's been done. You can give birth. You can fight. You can cause your family to be saved. You can stop a divorce. You can stand and not fall. You can declare over your generation's life. As a women you are the life of your home, you can birth ideas, dreams, hope, love, fidelity and so much more...The Bible is filled with women that were used by God in amazing ways, for example:

Deborah (Fighter): Judges 4:9:'And she said, I will surely go with you; nevertheless, the trip you take will not be for your glory, for the Lord will sell Sisera into the hand of a woman. And Deborah arose and went with Barak to Kedesh.'

Mary Magdalene (Faithful and so much more): John 19:25 :'But by the cross of Jesus stood His mother, His mother's sister, Mary the [wife] of Clopas, and Mary Magdalene.' (Notice all women)

The Samaritan Woman (Evangelist): John 4:39: 'Now numerous Samaritans from that town believed in and trusted in Him because of what the woman said when she declared and testified, He told me everything that I ever did.'

Esther (amazing): Esther 2:17: 'And the king loved Esther more than all the women, and she obtained grace and favor in his sight more than all the maidens, so that he set the royal crown on her head and made her queen instead of Vashti.'

Ja'el (warrior): Judges 5:26 (Amplified Bible):She put her [left] hand to the tent pin, and her right hand to the workmen's hammer. And with the wooden hammer she smote Sisera, she smote his head, yes, she struck and pierced his temple.'

Just to name a few.

So next time you don't understand what is going on or why your going through so much, stand up and say, "I now know why, because I can give birth to the next generation that will fight against you! Out of my womb come: the next Evangelist, the next Prophet, the next Pastor, the next Teacher, the next Apostle, the next one that will pierce the nail in Satan's temple like Ja'el. So watch out because I am still standing despite your attempts, I will continue to declare life, and I will make all what God has for me on this Earth a reality, in Jesus name. AMEN!"

Today, say a special prayer for the women all around the world, voice your prayer with understanding and revelation.

~TRANSFORMED~

2 Corinthians 3:18: (NKJ): "But we all, with unveiled face, beholding as in a mirror the glory of the Lord, are being transformed into the same image from glory to glory, just as by the Spirit of the Lord"

Metamorphosis is a biological process by which an animal physically develops after birth or hatching, involving a conspicuous and relatively abrupt change in the animal's body structure. Insects and other animals usually change habitat or behavior after metamorphosis. Do you see any similarities to a Christian? (after birth= born again, change habitat or behavior=what did you change?).

People often look in the mirror in different phases of their lives and begin to question their choices, their lives, their talents and other things. Some look back with regret, some look back with smiles, and some just think, 'I can't believe I'm still alive!' It takes different lengths of time for all of us to fully grasp the revelation of what we decide to do or not do, will effect our future in one way or another.

You can get an idea of how to gauge yourself on your transformation by answering one simple question... how much have I changed? In the past six months? In the last year? In the last five years? Some are just breaking out of their shell, others are at the cocoon phase and that's okay.

Standing with God truly will transform you, He will confront you when you're wrong and give you the strength to apologize, and He will show you love so you can show others. He will inspire you so you can inspire others. He does provide for you whatever you need so you can give it to others. He has it all for you today just ask in faith and receive in faith. You may not feel worthy at times but those are all lies, you are worthy He sent His Son to die for you and me just the same. So receive what you need whether its patience, love, wisdom, hope, to make the right choices; so when you look back you can say, "Wow I have come a long ways, I am not the same person I was just a year ago. I'm becoming a beautiful person full of life, freedom, wisdom and love. I am being transformed from glory to glory through Jesus name." Amen.

~Child~

Galatians 4:6-7 (Amplified Bible):6. And because you [really] are [His] sons, God has sent the [Holy] Spirit of His Son into our hearts, crying, Abba (Father)! Father! 7. Therefore, you are no longer a slave (bond servant) but a son; and if a son, then [it follows that you are] an heir by the aid of God, through Christ.

Words like grandchild, stepchild, adopted child, just to name a few, DO NOT exist in Kingdom of Heaven. Although these words are typically used to describe a child, a child status, or even to label a child; God never uses these words to describe you. You have never been any of these, you have always been a child of the Almighty God.

Funny thing about children is that each individual child has his/her own personality that is so unique and cannot be in anyway, shape, or form compared to another. This is very clear and apparent if you have children of your own, if you work with children, or just even know of children. Some are loud, some are quite, some will be obedient, some will disobey, some will fall, laugh and get up, while others will fall and need "mommy" or "daddy" to come get them. Think about what kind of child you were....

Regardless of how your parents were with you, whether they were great or not. Whether they abused you, ignored you, didn't defend you, or anything else, God is not like that.

He is concerned about your well-being, your heart, your future, your desires, and every other detail in your life.

He loves it when you run to Him all the time, with good news, bad news, questions, worries, plans, or anything else. What your doing is build a relationship with Him, your seeking His face and taking Him into account. So how much more will He take you into account?

Imagine how cool it is to know that the Creator of everything is with you, The Lion of the Tribe of Judah stands to fight for His children, the same God of Abraham, Isaac, and Moses is your DADDY!! He is the same from the past, the present, and the future, nothing can change Him, His heart, His love for you, nor His mercy.

Today take your identity back from the enemy, know who you are and I pray you have this revelation, it will change how you view yourself and your circumstances. Daddy loves you and is waiting to hear from you!

~Grafted~

Romans 11:17: But if some of the branches were broken off, while you, a wild olive shoot, were grafted in among them to share the richness [of the root and sap] of the olive tree.

Deuteronomy 14:2 (Amplified Bible): For you are a holy people [set apart] to the Lord your God; and the Lord has chosen you to be a peculiar people to Himself, above all the nations on the earth.

Grafting is a method widely used in agriculture and horticulture where the tissues of one plant are encouraged to fuse with those of another. The other plant is selected, cut at an angle, connected to the other tree, and held into place with bands until it has been fused with the other tree that will nourish it.

Grafting has been widely used in the secular world for centuries and not surprisingly God also uses it. It is estimated that their are approximately 15,500,000 Jews in the world today and through grafting their are an estimated 2-3 billion Christians in the world today. It wasn't until the New Testament that these promises were extended to the Gentiles and the term grafted was used to describe this process.

Secular grafting is similar to spiritual grafting, consider this, when the plant is selected it is then cut at an angle, banded together and the newly added branch begins to get fed and cared for by the main tree. The same water that feeds the original tree feeds also the new branch, the same things that protect the old tree protect the newly added branch. In other words all the benefits of the main tree are shared with the new branch.   The spiritual interpretation can be seen in Colossians 2:12 "[Thus you were circumcised when] you were buried with Him in [your] baptism, in which you were also raised with Him [to a new life] through [your] faith in the working of God [as displayed] when He raised Him up from the dead. "

Therefore it doesn't matter if your beginnings were small, your ending will not be. All those promises are for you the moment you receive Jesus as your Lord and Savior. You have been added to the Tree; the same promises that apply to Gods chosen apply to you, He chose you. Hang on the Tree and trust Him, He didn't graft you to let you down He grafted you to give you everything!

Today visualize yourself grafted to the Tree of God and begin to see Him as your protector, your water, your everything that you need as a branch, that Tree has it all for you. Just lay back and receive in faith.

~Omega~

Revelation 1:8 (Amplified Bible): I am the Alpha and the Omega, the Beginning and the End, says the Lord God, He Who is and Who was and Who is to come, the Almighty (the Ruler of all).

Matthew 21:22 (Amplified Bible): And whatever you ask for in prayer, having faith and [really] believing, you will receive.

Revelation 1:8 (Amplified Bible): I am the Alpha and the Omega, the Beginning and the End, says the Lord God, He Who is and Who was and Who is to come, the Almighty (the Ruler of all).

Matthew 21:22 (Amplified Bible): And whatever you ask for in prayer, having faith and [really] believing, you will receive.

Have you ever felt like your dreams have been shattered? That no matter how hard you push for something it feels like your swimming against the currents? Maybe there are things in your life you are too ashamed to speak about and you still don't know how to feel about it.

Depression is the leading mental health disorder in the United States, it is estimated that every year doctors treat some 4,000,000 to 8,000,000 Americans for it; about

250,000 of the cases require hospitalization. People suffer from depression for all types of reasons. Perhaps[s a loved one died, maybe your ashamed of your decisions and cant find away out, maybe your family is the reason why you suffer. The enemy will always come to accuse you and try to hold you down, you can count on that 1005, but you can also count on God 100%. Isn't He beautiful?

Regardless of what you may see in this world with your natural eyes, God sees things differently. You see, He already knew you, He made you, He knows your petitions, He knows your heart, and He loved you from the foundations of this Earth. Cry out to Him! Set yourself free! The Living Word of God says if you believe you will receive.

Today don't worry on the "how," the Virgin Mary didn't ask God "how" she was going to get pregnant, nor did David ask God "how" he was going to go from shepherd to king of all Israel. NO! They simply believed! Now you just have to ask in faith for your hearts petition, a way out, then believe, and God will manifest His Mercy, His Glory, His Supernatural Power to show you His final Word, to show you that when you are weak He is strong. Remember: When the world comes to knock you down just remember He is the Alpha and the Omega, He is the Beginning and the End; and He has your final answer. Whatever door He opens no man or situation can close, whatever door He closes no man or devil can open! BELIEVE! BELIEVE! BELIEVE! In Jesus name. Amen.

~BAITED~

James 1:14: But every person is tempted when he is drawn away, enticed and baited by his own evil desire (lust, passions).

1 John 4:4 (Amplified Bible): Little children, you are of God [you belong to Him] and have [already] defeated and overcome them [the agents of the antichrist], because He Who lives in you is greater (mightier) than he who is in the world.

It is relatively easy to catch fish, that is with the right bait. Fishermen will use the same type of bait over and over to achieve the same results, a fish. People who fish have to abide by certain laws that dictate if they can keep the fish or have to throw it back in the water. One of the factors that is looked at is if the size of a specific fish caught is to small then by law you must throw it back into the water. This is to ensure that the young fish may grow up and have offspring to continue being able to fish them in the future.

What would happen if their were fishermen that have no interest in protecting future generations of fish and continuously fished and fished with no concern of age nor laws? Well, there would be a decrease in the number of future fish produced and the delicate ecological system of that particular area would also be negatively impacted. So now the question is if you were a fish, what bait would make you lose your peace and cause you to sin? Peace may not sound as important as it is, consider the more extreme side of the spectrum and think about how many inmates had their peace taken from them for a moment; or how many drug addicts need to find peace to let that addiction go. The bait was placed and the fish was caught.

You see, the enemy is that fisherman that wants to bait you and the younger he is able to get you the better. When you are young either physically or spiritually it is easier to put paradigms and build strongholds in your mind and heart. Even seasoned Christians are in danger of losing there peace and in turn their blessing. The enemy waits to see what will bait you and then he tosses the line with the hook. He also knows that if he can bait you, it will be easier to take your generations because the delicate ecosystem (home) will be affected as well. The enemy has been casting his lines for centuries now and this is the result, people are constantly giving him legal right to be afflicted. Look around, read the news, watch the TV, look at family structure, its everywhere.

It may sound impossible to think that we can live without being tempted, and your right. Temptation is something we all have to deal with, even Jesus was tempted. The three times He was tempted He response back with "It is written...."

Today be reminded that "It is written... that stronger is He that is in you than he that is in the world!" Jesus already gave us the victory, He already gave you a way to have peace. You do not have to fall into temptation, you are stronger than you can possibly imagine because the Holy Spirit is in you the moment you receive Jesus as your Lord and Savior. There is so much freedom in knowing that you don't have to get upset, you don't have to live stressed out, you don't have to be addicted to anything, you don't have to be ashamed, and you don't have to bite the hook in your life! So for now on when the enemy comes to throw you bait, stand with the conviction that he will not steal your peace!

Prayer For You Today:

Father in the name of Jesus, Lord I pray that your people open their eyes and see what lays behind the bait. I pray that they can see the huge hook hidden that the enemy has planted for them. Father I pray that in those intense moments before a decision is made that the Holy Spirit stops them from falling into temptation. I pray for your people that they have peace and self-control in Jesus name. Amen.

~Architect~

Deuteronomy 30:19: I call heaven and earth to record this day against you, that I have set before you life and death, blessing and cursing: therefore choose life, that both thou and thy seed may live.

Matthew 12:37: For by your words you will be justified and acquitted, and by your words you will be condemned and sentenced.

Proverbs 18:21: Death and life are in the power of the tongue: and they that love it shall eat the fruit thereof.

Building a structure is a very complicated process and all parties involved have to work together in accord. The blueprint is the first thing that has to be created. During this phase everyone meets and decides on the structure, the materials, the costs and everything and everyone needed to build their idea. Building the foundation is the next step then everything else can be added afterwards. If your life were a building, what kind of building would you be? What kinds of words have been used to describe you? What have other people said about you? How have you edified yourself or your home?

The reality is that through your spoken words and inner thoughts life or death springs up. You have the power to bring up life through positive thoughts and words, or the power to create death by negative thoughts and hurtful words.

Its is amazing what can come out of our mouths, words that can bring someone to want to kill themselves or words that can bring a sickly soul back to life. What are your thoughts? What words are you using? Are you bringing words of life into your home, into your relationship, into your children?

We can't always depend on what other people say about us to continuously bring us life; we need to be able to bring ourselves life. How do we do that? Well you can do it on your own through the Bible also known as the Word of God. These are His Words and promises in our life that we can receive. He tells us what He says about us and all we have to do is declare it and believe it. It is the Living Word because you establish it; it lives according to your thoughts, words, and actions.

You can begin building life right now by praying and declaring the Word of God into your life and over your family. You also have the authority to cancel curses and non-edifying words spoken against you by canceling them in the name of Jesus, so they are not established in your life. On the same note you have the authority to receive and establish a blessing given to you, just by saying I receive it in the name of Jesus.

Today listen, really listen to your thoughts, listen to what others are saying, listen to what the media is saying, open your ears and become aware of what messages are really being put out there. It will surprise you. Then open your mouth and declare life.

My Prayer For You:
Lord in the name of Jesus I pray that you open your children's ears to the reality of what is being confessed over them. I declare in the name of Jesus that today whatever has been spoken over you to harm you, to curse you, or to make you captive falls at your feet and I declare you free. In Jesus name. Amen.

~Doors~

1 Corinthians 3:16 (King James Version): 16 Know ye not that ye are the temple of God, and that the Spirit of God dwelleth in you?

Luke 11:24-26 (Amplified Bible): When the unclean spirit has gone out of a person, it roams through waterless places in search [of a place] of rest (release, refreshment, ease); and finding none it says, I will go back to my house from which I came. **25** And when it arrives, it finds [the place] swept and put in order and furnished and decorated. **26** And it goes and brings other spirits, seven [of them], more evil than itself, and they enter in, settle down, and dwell there; and the last state of that person is worse than the first.

Job 5:17 (Amplified Bible): 17 Happy and fortunate is the man whom God reproves; so do not despise or reject the correction of the Almighty.

Doors are like valves, an open valve allows things in and a closed valve does not. A door can be opened with a key, a code, the lock can be picked, and a door can also be forced opened. There are different levels of security that can be put on a door to ensure safety, for example: a lock, a dead bolt, a security system, a Rottweiler...etc. How do you protect your material things?

There are laws in different countries by various titles that allow the occupant of a home to keep the home if the owner does not claim it for a certain amount of years depending in what country. In other words, the occupant would have legal right to keep a house that was not theirs. If we are a temple then that means we also must have and occupant (ideally the Holy Spirit) and doors, a way in and a way out. If we are free in Jesus it is still up to us to remain free. We may have the house clean, the bumper sticker on our car, the Christian pin on our shirt, but if the house is empty it can be overtaken again but this time the damage will be worse.

You may wonder what open these doors, but you may already know the answer, sin. You see every time we sin we give the enemy legal right into our house. He can also hold the door open and invite others to play on your emotions, on your health, on anything because his foot is in the door. So if you are free in this world because you feel you can do anything, are your really free because you then have to deal with the consequences, like for instance: the "What do I do now," the "How did I get into this?," the "Who do I call for help," the "If anyone found out," the "I wonder what this STD test will say," the "How am I going to pay for this now," just to name a few.

If God corrects you and you follow His commandments, that if you notice are really for your own good, do you think you will be free? Freedom is more than the choice to do something you feel like doing, freedom is also a feeling, for example: feeling free of guilt, free of consequence, free of addiction, free of captivity, free to be all that He has made you to be, free to try, free to say I love you, free to say your sorry, free to love others, free to ask for help, DRAMA-FREE, just to name a few.

Today, if you want to be free you have to close the doors. Ignorance is also a door. Monitor your temple with the alarm systems God gave you: intimacy with Him and prayer, praise and worship, the Bible, fasting, a congregation. Its not easy but "NO" can save your life both physically and spiritually.

My Prayer For You:

Father, in the name of Jesus I pray over your children declaring that they are ready for You to reveal to them what doors they have opened in their lives. Father I pray that You give us all the strength to slam shut those doors and to truly be free. Thank You because You are not the one who accuses us, You are the One who forgives us. In Jesus name. Amen.

~Seat~

Matthew 11:28: Come to Me, all you who labor and are heavy-laden and overburdened, and I will cause you to rest. [I will ease and relieve and refresh your souls.]

Hebrews 11:1: NOW FAITH is the assurance (the confirmation, the title deed) of the things [we] hope for, being the proof of things [we] do not see and the conviction of their reality.

> Does your faith move God enough for Him to
> act on your behalf?

Sitting down is one of the most common positions we will find ourselves in. Whether you are working, waiting, wondering, or whatever else, sitting down is something that we all naturally do. If the seat looks like it has all its legs and its not incredible dirty chances are it's a good candidate to rest on. The more appealing the seat looks the more you may want to sit down and maybe even kick your feet up for a while. It's easy to sit down on something that our natural eyes can see. Is it just as easy to have faith in something we can't see or didn't see?

The Bible is a compilation of stories told by others to help us to see that God is real. The stories move from person to person, situations to situations and its clear that God is moved by Faith. So the question is, where is your faith? In your own abilities? In someone else's abilities? On a Lotto ticket? Where?

Your faith is knowing that you can close your eyes, breath in, kick back, and know that God loves you more than a seat ever could. If you do what you can and to the best of your abilities and have faith in Him, God will do what you can't do, through His limitlessness abilities.

Today sit down on a chair, put your feet up, and picture that chair being a refuge for your soul. The same way you are being held up off the floor trusting a chair, put your trust in God and let Him give you rest.

~KEYS~

Revelation 1:18: And the Ever-living One [I am living in the eternity of the eternities]. I died, but see, I am alive forevermore; and I possess the keys of death.

Matthew 16:19: I will give you the keys of the kingdom of heaven; and whatever you bind (declare to be improper and unlawful) on earth must be what is already bound in heaven; and whatever you loose (declare lawful) on earth must be what is already loosed in heaven.

There was a plague that originated in South America and then began to spread to Central America. The nations began to sanction and quarantine individuals that had the symptoms of the plague in a feudal attempt to stop the spread. However it was all in vain. The plague continued to spread, showing up in various parts in Europe, the Americas, Africa, Asia and the number of lives lost was staggering and growing.

The world's scientist and doctors gathered together and found a weak point in the virus. The only problem was finding someone who had the necessary ingredients in their blood to then duplicate it. At the news of this discovery everyone was exited, hope had been restored. The nations declared a mandatory blood analysis for all adults. Months later hope began to fade again, not one person had the cure in their blood.

Then the nations declared another mandatory blood analysis but this time for all children and infants. Within a month a little girl was discovered to have the cure. Then nations cheered and the family was exited to know that they would be the ones that would save the world. However their victory was short-lived at discovering that they would have to allow their daughter to die for the world to live. At discovering the need for the sacrifice, the father immediately cried out and would not allow that to happen. As he hugged his daughter he cried, and she raised her tiny body up and wiped her fathers tears and said, "But daddy, I can save them, I will do this." She smiled and her father broke down. Her mother was silent and in pain, knowing this was the only option. THERE EXISTED NO OTHER OPTION.

The little girl rose up and went with the doctors and scientist who were all crying and gave her life up to save the world. It only took a matter of months before the world population was healed from the plague and hope was restored. The people were so grateful and full of life again that it was declared that day to be a world holiday.

A year later a stadium was rented to celebrate the little girls life in remembrance of her and her families sacrifice. It was expected that millions of people from all nations would come and give homage, however as the hours went by only about seventy people showed up. Some would show up for a little bit and leave, others just had to many things to do that day, while yet others didn't see that it was her that saved them and invented some story about how they were saved by x, y and z.

Today on this day that we mourn the death of our Lord and Savior, we are actually celebrating the victory over the enemy. On this day two thousand years ago, Jesus shook hell and Earth and with all authority delegated from God Himself, Jesus shamed Satan, and took back the keys that Adam and Eve had legally given up. Thank you for your sacrifice Jesus, I will be at the stadium!

~PERFECT~

Deuteronomy 32:4 : He is the Rock, His work is perfect, for all His ways are law and justice. A God of faithfulness without breach or deviation, just and right is He.

Leviticus 22:21 : And whoever offers a sacrifice of peace offering to the Lord to make a special vow to the Lord or for a freewill offering from the herd or from the flock must bring what is **perfect** to be accepted; there shall be no blemish in it.

1 John 4:9 : In this the love of God was made manifest (displayed) where we are concerned: in that God sent His Son, the only begotten or unique [Son], into the world so that we might live through Him.

Perfect sacrifice?

God is a perfect God and He is perfect in His laws, so much so that even though He made them He does not break them. Centuries back before Jesus was born the Israelites had to sacrifice animals for many reasons, including peace offerings or to remove the debt of sin. Being how the consequence of sin is death, something had to die in order for that person to be redeemed.

Throughout the Bible many examples are given of peoples sacrifices. At times God was pleased because it was the best possible first fruits; and at other times He was displeased because it was the last of the bunch. You see, God has emotions He is not a God who just sits on a throne and passes judgment. When you offer something to Him, He sees it and knows your heart. Can you see His sacrifice and know His heart?

From all the angels in the heavens, from all the archangels in the heavens, or from any willing individual already on Earth, God chose the best He had. He chose a perfect, blemish-less, uncorrupted, holy, sanctified sacrifice to show us His heart. He chose His first-born Son to take away a debt that we could not pay so we could live. His sacrifice was so powerful that even unto this day a truly repented sinner can be redeemed no matter what sins have been committed.

Today meditate on Gods sacrifice, ask the Holy Spirit for a revelation of His heart, and what this weekend really represents. He is here for you with arms wide open regardless of your sins. This is what its all about...you!

~Psalm 23 (Amplified Bible)~

A Psalm of David.

1 THE LORD is my Shepherd [to feed, guide,
and shield me], I shall not lack.
2 He makes me lie down in [fresh, tender] green pastures;
He leads me beside the still and restful waters.
3 He refreshes and restores my life (my self);
He leads me in the paths of righteousness [uprightness and
right standing with Him--not for my earning it,
but] for His name's sake.
4 Yes, though I walk through the [deep, sunless]
valley of the shadow of death, I will fear or dread no evil,
for You are with me; Your rod [to protect] and
Your staff [to guide], they comfort me.
5 You prepare a table before me in the presence of my
enemies. You anoint my head with oil;
my [brimming] cup runs over.
6 Surely or only goodness, mercy, and unfailing
love shall follow me all the days of my life, and
through the length of my days the house of the Lord
[and His presence] shall be my dwelling place.

*Today know that He lives, He is resurrected, and He is
waiting for you to rest in Him.*

~Hands~

Deuteronomy 7:19: The great trials which your eyes saw, the signs, the wonders, the mighty hand and the outstretched arm by which the Lord your God brought you out. So shall the Lord your God do to all the people of whom you are afraid.

Numbers 11:23 (Amplified Bible): The Lord said to Moses, Has the Lord's hand (His ability and power) become short (thwarted and inadequate)? You shall see now whether My word shall come to pass for you or not.

Psalm 28:2 : Hear the voice of my supplication as I cry to You for help, as I lift up my hands toward Your innermost sanctuary (the Holy of Holies).

There was a little boy who was playing outside and fell down. He cried out for help and couldn't get up because his leg was hurting. His mother drove past him and saw him. She immediately parked the car and went to him. She stretched out her hand to help him, but instead of reaching for his mom, he reached down to push himself off the ground. He wiped his tears and wiped off the dirt from his jeans. His mother asked, "I was here to pick you up, why didn't you take my hand?"

Sometimes we find ourselves trying to get up on our own during a situation were you have nowhere to turn to, or so it seems. In those feelings of insecurity you may feel that you can somehow resolve the problem on your own and in your strength. The truth of the matter is that there always is a hand outreached and extended to you. An Almighty Hand that longs to feel your hand in His.

King David had several revelations of how Gods mighty hand had covered him in the past and delivered him from death on several occasions. He knew that if He just put his hands up like a child reaching for his Daddy, He was going to be just fine. And He was.

When you feel the worldly pressures, reach up with your hands far stretched and cry out to God, saying "Daddy." Know that His hand is Almighty and always ready to hold yours. You are not alone, no matter how many times you fall.

~EARTH~

Genesis 1:26: God said, Let Us [Father, Son, and Holy Spirit] make mankind in Our image, after Our likeness, and let them have complete authority over the fish of the sea, the birds of the air, the [tame] beasts, and over all of the earth, and over everything that creeps upon the earth.

Genesis 1:28: And God blessed them and said to them, Be fruitful, multiply, and fill the earth, and subdue it [using all its vast resources in the service of God and man]; and have dominion over the fish of the sea, the birds of the air, and over every living creature that moves upon the earth.

It's unfortunate that many hold different views on what dominion is and who should have dominion over what. Although it is not difficult to determine what should not be done just out plain common sense or compassion; it appears many still feel they have the right to exercise abuse over the Earth and it's animals. There are many animals that are endangered today that are expected to be extinct with in a few years, for example the: Mountain Gorilla, Bactrian Camel, Ethiopian Wolf, Javan Rhino, Leatherback Sea Turtle, Northern White Rhinoceros, Philippine Eagle, Brown Spider Monkey, California Condor, Island Fox, Black Rhinoceros, Chinese Alligator, etc.

It may seem hopeless for these species listed above to make a come back, however their are many animals that have in the past made it off the critically endangered animal list. You may wonder what this has to do with being spiritual, but it does. God said for us to have dominion over the Earth, and we do. Everyday we decide as individuals if we are going to purchase environmentally safe to eat foods, detergents, and other goods. We also can decide if we are going to recycle and to what extent we are committed to that. We can also decide if we are going to litter or not. There are many things as individuals we can do. I urge you to ask God to give you guidance in this area. We need to work together to ensure our generations receive from us an inheritance that is good.

Today I encourage you to look around and be compelled to do something different for God, sometimes its not just about a person, its about the whole package; Earth and all.

My Prayer For You:
Father in the name of Jesus, Lord I pray that your children receive a revelation that changes strongholds and paradigms. Father I pray that people become more and more environmentally aware and savvy. Lord I pray that the leaders around the world receive wisdom from above on how to handle our worldly environmental crisis. Let your healing hand bring life to were life has been uprooted. In Jesus name. Amen.

~Choice~

Deuteronomy 4:9: Only take heed, and guard your life diligently, lest you forget the things which your eyes have seen and lest they depart from your [mind and] heart all the days of your life. Teach them to your children and your children's children--

Deuteronomy 5:9: You shall not bow down to them or serve them; for I, the Lord your God, am a jealous God, visiting the iniquity of the fathers upon the children to the third and fourth generations of those who hate Me,

There was a story about a little boy who was 5 years old whose father was being prosecuted for child abuse. The fathers pleads not guilty for the charges and he claims that the child insisted that he wanted to have his whole entire body covered with tattoos. In the end the child had over 75% of his body covered with everything and anything he wanted. It obviously did not occur to the father that as the boy grew up the tattoos would get stretched out and become deformed. Nor did it occur to his father that perhaps it would be difficult for the child to look for a job when he became an adult, because he had his whole face, neck, and head covered with tattoos. So the question is would you allow a child to make these types of decisions that would affect the rest of their lives? Would you allow a child to make their own spiritual decisions?

It is naturally in our flesh to want to be comfortable and spend the extra time that we have to relax and unwind. Is this passive attitude helping or hurting our future generations? I suggest we take a look around. It appears that if we don't teach them the Word of God by being an example and by actually reading it to them, we can't count on others to do it for us, so how will they learn? In the book of Revelations/ Apocalypse it is really clear that the times will be getting worse and if you can see, it already is. What foundations are you leaving your future generations to keep them strong when those days come? Are you willing to risk their futures by not showing them the true Word of God.

This is obviously very important to God, He mentions future generations, generational blessings, and generational cursing very often. Is it then fair to leave your child's spirit to their own devices?

Today, think about what tools are you leaving your generations to fight with when you are called to be with the Lord. Will your children be strong with the fruits of the Holy Spirit, will they have communion with God, will they know Him as their heavenly Daddy that is always with them, loves them, and will forgive them? Or will you leave them with no tools and on the opposite side for example: will they be easily tempted, hurt by the rejections of this world, feel as though no one is their for them, or no one loves them? It's not easy and sometimes it takes time for them to get it, but it's worth it.

~Measurements~

Proverbs 24:16 (Amplified Bible): For a righteous man falls seven times and rises again, but the wicked are overthrown by calamity.

Romans 3:23-25 (Amplified Bible): Since all have sinned and are falling short of the honor and glory which God bestows and receives. **24** [All] are justified and made upright and in right standing with God, freely and gratuitously by His grace (His unmerited favor and mercy), through the redemption which is [provided] in Christ Jesus, **25** Whom God put forward before the eyes of all] as a mercy seat and propitiation by His blood [the cleansing and life-giving sacrifice of atonement and reconciliation, to be received] through faith. This was to show God's righteousness, because in His divine forbearance He had passed over and ignored former sins without punishment.

Nothing can surprise God, He already knows each and every mistake we have made and will make. The only one Worthy to be a sacrifice was Jesus both in the past and in present time. Although He never fell by sinning, He did fall while holding the cross. How heavy is your cross? Do you feel like you are falling, about to fall, or did you already fall?

We all fall into sin. We all battle different battles but its the same struggling feelings. A drug addict's struggle is the same as a hopelessly in love person who wants to engage in fornication with their significant other. Its truly the same black and white line that we all walk on, do we fall into temptation or not.

The more you choose to carry your cross to follow Jesus, the more temptation you will have, but the more grace you will have to have victory. God shows us that there is nothing we could ever do or say that would or could cover our ransom. He also shows us that we cannot measure up to the perfection that is Jesus, it was and is always His blood that covers our lack; and that's were we need to go back to when we fall. To His blood, once forgiven, repent and turn from your temptation.

Today ask the Holy Spirit to show you were you are weak and to help you walk over those things designed by the enemy to cause you to fall. Remember the Holy Spirit confronts you about your sin, but its the enemy who convicts you and makes you feel guilty and unworthy, go to God and get right with Him.

My Prayer for you:

Holy Father in the heavens above, I pray that you look at us today with eyes of forgiveness and touch our souls with hands of mercy. Your compassion and love for us is abundant, were we fail your love and grace abundantly covers us. Father, we can never measure up to the perfect statue of Jesus, but His blood rises in our defense to cover our shortcomings. That precious blood that was spilled for our ransom, by that blood we continue to be justified and made righteous. Forgive us our sins whether conscious or unconscious, whether in thought or by actions. Father I remind you that by His blood, we have entrance into your Holiest place to receive healing, forgiveness and to tell You thank You, we will try better next time, and we love You with all our being. In Jesus name. Amen

Self-Liberation:

In the name of Jesus I declare myself free, I declare that any and all things that tempt me to fall are removed from my path. I rebuke in the name of Jesus any unclean being that influences my mind or body. I rip out in the name of Jesus and with God's mighty hand all things planted in my soul that God did not plant. Spirit of guilt, spirit of condemnation, spirit of shame, (whatever else the Holy Spirit brings to mind), I bind you and send you all to dry lands of captivity were you cannot rise up against me nor my generations in Jesus name. Now I ask that the Holy Spirit fill me up with healing, with love, and with anything else I need in order for me to walk in the Spirit and not the flesh. Through Jesus name. Amen.

~Judging~

Luke 6:37: Judge not, and ye shall not be judged: condemn not, and ye shall not be condemned: forgive, and ye shall be forgiven:

Romans 2:1 (Amplified Bible): THEREFORE YOU have no excuse or defense or justification, O man, whoever you are who judges and condemns another. For in posing as judge and passing sentence on another, you condemn yourself, because you who judge are habitually practicing the very same things [that you censure and denounce].

Proverbs 10:12 (Amplified Bible): Hatred stirs up contentions, but love covers all transgressions.

There is a big difference between judging a person and correcting a person. We are called to identify sin and part ways from it, to help those in darkness to see light. The authorities of the world have their own judicial system in place to deal with law breakers and persons found guilty of a crime; but consider this, how many of those found guilty are really innocent?

Unwillingly at times, or purposely we seem to create jails for others by passing judgment, gossiping, and criticizing. These things may cause others to feel ostracized, abandoned, hated, and maybe even suicidal. Its difficult to imagine what goes on in a persons mind, what their thought patterns are like, or even to imagine how much that person can take before they just can't take anymore.

Everyone needs to vent now and then, or discuss a situation when you are looking for a real solution, however their needs to be an increased awareness of the purpose of the conversation. You can ask yourself some basic questions like: is this conversation going to help me or make the situation or my feelings better or worse, is this person going to tell everyone else what I am about to say, can I trust this person to give me the best possible advice on a situation, does this person have my best interest at heart, or am I going to be judged instead of understood with this person, to get a better understanding of the people you speak with, and the nature of your conversation. Always keep in mind if you are going to discuss something, their are people that are better suited to talk to then others, for example if you are building a home will you discuss your layout with the town baker or with an architect? Extend the same to others, if someone came to you and asked for advice and you do not have a clue, refer them to someone else that may be better suited to help them. Or if someone wanted to gossip or criticize you do not have to lend them your ears, nor continue spreading the news to another person.

Today ask God for wisdom to know whom you should discuss what with, and ask Him to also guard your mind and mouth to prevent judging others. If you see a person going down the wrong path, ask God for words of wisdom to address the situation before you speak to them in order to ensure its done with love and patience.

My Prayer For You:

Heavenly Father, I come to you today Lord to give you thanks and to exalt Your name. Your mercies are many and Your Hand is great, I love You. I ask Father that You open our understanding, that You give us Your eyes to see how You see. I pray that You give us Your heart to feel what You feel. Lord I ask that today You give us wisdom to seek out advice, that You put a guard over our mouths so we don't spew venom from our conversations. I pray that You show us how to correct in love and not in angry judgment. Lord show us how to cover our brothers weakness with love. Daddy help us all. In Jesus name. Amen.

~PROMISES~

Psalm 12:6: The words and **promises** of the Lord are pure words, like silver refined in an earthen furnace, purified seven times over.

Jeremiah 29:11 (Amplified Bible): For I know the thoughts and plans that I have for you, says the Lord, thoughts and plans for welfare and peace and not for evil, to give you hope in your final outcome.

Romans 8:28 (Amplified Bible): We are assured and know that [God being a partner in their labor] all things work together and are [fitting into a plan] for good to and for those who love God and are called according to [His] design and purpose.

Jeremiah 29:12 (Amplified Bible): Then you will call upon Me, and you will come and pray to Me, and I will hear and heed you

Today simply meditate on His Words and know that if He promised it, it will happen.

~91~

Psalm 91

1 HE WHO dwells in the secret place of the Most High
shall remain stable and fixed under the shadow of the
Almighty [Whose power no foe can withstand].
2 I will say of the Lord, He is my Refuge and
my Fortress, my God; on Him I lean and rely, and
in Him I [confidently] trust!
3 For [then] He will deliver you from the snare of the
fowler and from the deadly pestilence.
4 [Then] He will cover you with His pinions, and
under His wings shall you trust and find refuge;
His truth and His faithfulness are a shield and a buckler.
5 You shall not be afraid of the terror of the night,
nor of the arrow (the evil plots and
slanders of the wicked) that flies by day,
6 Nor of the pestilence that stalks in darkness,
nor of the destruction and sudden death that
surprise and lay waste at noonday.
7 A thousand may fall at your side, and ten thousand at
your right hand, but it shall not come near you.
8 Only a spectator shall you be [yourself inaccessible in the
secret place of the Most High] as you witness the
reward of the wicked.

9 Because you have made the Lord your refuge, and the
Most High your dwelling place,
10 There shall no evil befall you, nor any plague or
calamity come near your tent.
11 For He will give His angels [especial]
charge over you to accompany and defend and
preserve you in all your ways [of obedience and service].
12 They shall bear you up on their hands,
lest you dash your foot against a stone.
13 You shall tread upon the lion and adder;
the young lion and the serpent
shall you trample underfoot.

God answers David back saying:

14 Because he has set his love upon Me, therefore will I
deliver him; I will set him on high, because he knows and
understands My name [has a personal knowledge of
My mercy, love, and kindness--trusts and relies on Me,
knowing I will never forsake him, no, never].
15 He shall call upon Me, and I will answer him;
I will be with him in trouble, I will deliver him and
honor him.
16 With long life will I satisfy him and
how him My salvation.

Today be passionate about expressing your feelings to God, ask the Holy Spirit to bring you fire and passion in your life and in prayer. Write your own psalms and poems about what God has done for you, or how He has delivered you. Those reminders will keep you strong when you feel weak, they will also give you hope when you feel hopeless. Feel that Holy Fire burn inside of you as you write, and wait for Him to answer you back. You may be surprised but God is a passionate God and He is perfectly poetic!

~STRANGE~

Leviticus 10:1-3: 1 AND NADAB and Abihu, the sons of Aaron, each took his censer and put fire in it, and put incense on it, and offered strange and unholy fire before the Lord, as He had not commanded them. **2** And there came forth fire from before the Lord and killed them, and they died before the Lord. **3.** Then Moses said to Aaron, This is what the Lord meant when He said, I [and My will, not their own] will be acknowledged as hallowed by those who come near Me, and before all the people I will be honored. And Aaron said nothing.

1Samuel 13:14 (Amplified Bible): 14 But now your kingdom shall not continue; the Lord has sought out [David] a man after His own heart, and the Lord has commanded him to be prince and ruler over His people, because you have not kept what the Lord commanded you.

2Samuel 6:14-16 (Amplified Bible): 14 And David danced before the Lord with all his might, clad in a linen ephod [a priest's upper garment].**15** So David and all the house of Israel brought up the ark of the Lord with shouting and with the sound of the trumpet. **16** As the ark of the Lord came into the City of David, Michal, Saul's daughter [David's wife], looked out of the window and saw King David leaping and dancing before the Lord, and she despised him in her heart.

If you ever tried to buy something from a vending machine you would know that there are certain dollar bills or cents that are accepted in the machine. You may try to put a penny in it, but it will get rejected. You could also have more than enough for the item, like a hundred dollar bill, but even that will be rejected. You need the right type of change to get what you want from the vending machine.

In the scripture above about the two priest that died, they had offered God "strange fire," in other words they tried to worship God in front of the Tabernacle in their own way and died instantly. Although we no longer have to worship in front of the Tabernacle we are still in danger of dying, spiritually that is. Have you ever seen Christians that are spiritually blocked, or that feel alone, or that do so much work in a church but can't see Gods glory; kind of like offering up that hundred dollar bill to the vending machine, doing so much then being rejected. They are somewhat easy to recognize and typically say things like: "I worship God my way," or "When He makes my wishes come true then I will be thankful," or "What will people think if I worship God?" or "I'll just keep doing all these works for the church because God likes that."

Although Gods tabernacle is not in front of us, He sees your heart and He sees your worship. Is your worship a sweet smelling offering of gratitude, love, is it a real worship, or is it more of an emotionless offer before the King, before the One who made heaven and Earth, before the One who fights your battles?

Interestingly enough when visitors visit different types of churches, that person may be on fire dancing in Gods presence and that church may think, "What is wrong with that person," while in other churches they are all dancing in His presence and the visitor is thinking, "What are they doing, they are all crazy," while the church community is thinking, "Why is that person not joining in." Although we may all come from a different spiritual background, the question is are your prayers being answered? Are you able to see Gods 'super naturalness' in your life? Can you feel His presence? If you answered no, ask yourself this, "If God was a vending machine, am I offering the right type of coins (worship)?"

In the second example when King David danced in the Lords presence, he danced until he was in his boxer's, and in front of all of Jerusalem with shouts of joy and victory. Surely enough there will be people who do not understand what you are doing like David's wife, however your relationship with God is a personal one. Some may even become jealous because they see what God is doing in your life, or they may want to be able to do what you can do in prayer or worship, either way do not allow that to stop you from getting your blessing. David offered up the right type of offering to God, and went from shepherd boy to King of the Israelites. God Himself even said "David, a man after My own heart."

Today offer up a worship worthy of your petitions, that is according to Gods will (which is found in the Bible), and wait. It won't be long before the perfume of your worship hits Gods nose, and when He inhales your offering, He will exhale His glory over you and your life.

~Hospital~

Proverbs 17:9 (New Living Translation): Love prospers when a fault is forgiven, but dwelling on it separates close friends.

Jeremiah 17:9-10 (Amplified Bible): 9 The heart is deceitful above all things, and it is exceedingly perverse and corrupt and severely, mortally sick! Who can know it [perceive, understand, be acquainted with his own heart and mind]? **10** I the Lord search the mind, I try the heart, even to give to every man according to his ways, according to the fruit of his doings

Capitalistic societies naturally create illusions of wealth behind trademarks and material luxuries. Many times average people fall into debt trying to create the illusion of success and status. In the long run it not only drains the person but it also drains the bank accounts and the quality of life of that individual. Many divorces are caused by financial strains as well. Keeping up with the Jones is very difficult and dangerous both in the secular world and in the spiritual world.

The same way a person may work to try to create an illusion of success in the secular world, many Christians work to create a similar illusion; the illusion of forgiveness, holiness, self control, spirituality, and others.

Unfortunately many people are deceived when they join a church, by their own standards and expectations. You see a church is like a hospital were the sick go to get healed, then in turn where those that were healed go to heal others while still being a work in progress.

The enemy constantly attacks churches with gossip, criticism, and judgment, amongst so much more different tactics; unfortunately that may be a turn off for many to join a congregation. Many people go on fire for God to a church and see that the pastor is not doing this or that, or that the people are this and that, but God didn't call you to judge. No, God called you to get congregated, to be part of group that with all its imperfections loves you and is there for you. You can't control others but you can control yourself, you don't have to listen to the gossip, you can intercede for the pastors, you can even ask God to move you if you know He wants you somewhere else.

There is so much freedom not living for illusions and realizing your own imperfections. Have compassion on those that have not understood their own need for light in those areas you already have victory over. You'll realize that truly there are areas in your life that need light as well, and then pray that there will be someone there to help you that is as compassionate as you are.

Truly forgive those that need to be forgiven, don't dwell on past faults of your brothers and sisters, be true to the Gospel, and know that we struggle daily with our own heart and emotions.

Today, reflect back and name those persons who have hurt you, forgive them, let them go, and pray for them. Sometimes we are unexpectedly hurt by an offense, a misunderstanding or something along those lines, it happens at work, in the family, everywhere. Offenses are bound to happen and sometimes God is simply testing your heart so you can see what is in it. Be a blessing were you go until God calls you somewhere else.

~Cockatiel~

Philippians 2:9 (King James Version): 9 Wherefore God also hath highly exalted him, and given him a name which is above every name:

Matthew 7:22-23 (Amplified Bible): 22 Many will say to Me on that day, Lord, Lord, have we not prophesied in Your name and driven out demons in Your name and done many mighty works in Your name? **23** And then I will say to them openly (publicly), I never knew you; depart from Me, you who act wickedly [disregarding My commands].

Mark 16:17 (Amplified Bible): 17 And these attesting signs will accompany those who believe: in My name they will drive out demons; they will speak in new languages;

A variety of birds can be taught to speak such as the Cockatiel, the African Grey parrot, and others. The bird that holds the record for speaking has over 1,700 words in his repertoire. The trainer must spend many hours working with the bird and be very patient. Do you think the bird understands what it is saying? If they are not responding to the queues that they were taught could they have a conversation?

The name Jesus is simply a word, some say it casually, some say it intertwined with curse words, and some just don't say it. Some mothers even name their children Jesus. It is just a word that you can even teach a bird to say over and over again.

When referring to God's Son, however the name truly does have so much power behind it. So much so that the name alone will be accounted for "many mighty works" done by people who are not even children of God. The type of power behind Jesus name is so very real. People who preach a false doctrine in His name will pay a severe price for leading His sheep astray. People who follow a false doctrine will also be subjected to judgment because ignorance does not excuse you. You are responsible for: educating yourself with the truth, searching out Gods face, desiring intimacy with Him, and having communion with Him, nobody else is. If you need a revelation ask Him for one, ask Him to convince you of His existence, if you don't feel Him, ask Him for a touch. Ask and you shall receive.

His name combined with revelation of who He is and knowledge of what He has given you (Holy Spirit, authority, etc.) will launch you into a new spiritual level. When you pray you will not be a Cockatiel simply repeating words with no authority or power.

If you truly walk with Him as His child, then truly you will be doing His will and He will be with you. You will not be scared to face any adversary because you will know He is with you. You too will be able to do mighty works based on your gifts and measure of faith.

Today, say out loud to establish it, "I am not a Cockatiel, when I pray I penetrate the heavens with my worship and petitions. In Jesus name I ask for a revelation that breaks strongholds in my mind and heart. I need a touch; I need You God to show me that you are with me. Show me the power and authority that has been dormant in me that You gave me from even before my birth. Show me the power of His name. In Jesus name. Amen."

~Kissed~

Luke 22:46-51 (Amplified Bible): 46 And He said to them, Why do you sleep? Get up and pray that you may not enter [at all] into temptation. **47** And while He was still speaking, behold, there came a crowd, and the man called Judas, one of the Twelve [apostles], was going before [leading] them. He drew near to Jesus to kiss Him, **48** But Jesus said to him, Judas! Would you betray and deliver up the Son of Man with a kiss? **49** And when those who were around Him saw what was about to happen, they said, Lord, shall we strike with the sword? **50** And one of them struck the bondservant of the high priest and cut off his ear, the right one. **51** But Jesus said, Permit them to go so far [as to seize Me]. And He touched the little (insignificant) ear and healed him.

Betrayed by a kiss, of all things. Judas was with Jesus and saw all the miracles He did for three years, and yet that was not enough to stop him from betraying Him. Although we are not God, we are the children of God and we all will be betrayed at some point. Many people walk this world hurt, jaded, guarded, and with walls around them built out of a need for protection. The quality of their relational life is very poor and some can't see outside their own needs to help others because of the fear of getting hurt again.

There are few people who have truly understood the idea that they are not the only ones subjected to betrayal. Living with a victim mentality continuously makes you a victim. Victims take on many forms, once I heard of a young man who had tattooed "never again" on his forearm. When asked, "What was never again?" He replied, "I'm never falling in love again." How sad that is to be so young and so unwilling to give anyone else another chance. How can someone hold something against someone else who did no harm based on their past? Surprisingly enough it's very possible and easily done.

Monitoring our thoughts and accepting correction helps us get past any phase of betrayal, whether you were the one doing the betraying, about to do the betraying, or the one getting over a Judas kiss. It hurts when things like this happen, many people seek professional help, pastoral counseling or other outside sources to help with the healing process.

Others react how Peter reacted with the sword in hand ready to defend his heart (Jesus). However Jesus reacted differently, He told Peter to put the sword away and healed the servants' ear that Peter had just cut off. Why do you think Jesus said to them to get up and pray so they don't fall into temptation? What was the temptation? Perhaps it was the temptation to defend Jesus by hurting or killing another person, or perhaps it was the temptation to hold resentment and unforgiveness towards Judas. As you know having resentment and unforgiveness stops the flow of the Holy Spirit, thus your gifts and calling, making a soft heart hard and not allowing you to feel compassion nor love in the truest and most potent form.

How do you stop from becoming jaded? Well God guards everything but your heart, that is your free will. You guard your heart by understanding that people will always betray you, but that you tried your best from the beginning to do the right thing. Its very different going into Gods throne saying, "God I tried, it didn't work, heal me," than saying, "God I didn't even give it a chance and now I am so bitter, and sometimes I don't even think Your real because if You were this never would have happened to me." Those are two extreme examples, but were do you fall?

Its okay to be vulnerable Jesus was, He didn't walk around with bodyguards or guard dogs. He simply moved with compassion and understanding, He walked in love and passion for us and for God. He knew He was going to be turned in and betrayed, it had been the plan from the beginning and even prophesied hundreds of years before He was born. The question is how did the guards catch Him, how did the situation catch Him? The answer is, in prayer, He was already strengthen for when Judas was going to betray Him. Are you strengthened?

Today strengthen yourself, betrayal comes from the most unexpected corners. It came to Jesus in the form of one of His disciples. Pray, ask God to reveal to you the hearts of the people around you so it's not so unexpected. Remember that from what comes out of the mouth is what flows in the heart.

Prayer For You:

Father in the name of Jesus, Lord I pray that you heal those battle scars left in your people's hearts by the enemy. Father I pray that this word gives your children revelation to live life passionately and full of compassion towards one another. Lord I pray that you reveal to them the hearts of those around them so they can foresee the other persons intentions and pray for wisdom and strength. Lord open the mouths of those looking to do them harm because from the mouth lies what is in the heart. Give us all strength and understanding to keep going on this walk with you, lest we fall short of Your forgiveness. Clean our souls and our hearts, make us wise when selecting friends, partners, husbands, and wives. In Jesus name. Amen.

~MILESTONE~

Isaiah 64:8(Amplified Bible): 8 Yet, O Lord, You are our Father; we are the clay, and You our Potter, and we all are the work of Your hand.

Zechariah 13:8-9 (Amplified Bible): 9 And I will bring the third part through the fire, and will refine them as silver is refined and will test them as gold is tested. They will call on My name, and I will hear and answer them. I will say, It is My people; and they will say, The Lord is my God.

Isaiah 43:2 (Amplified Bible): 2 When you pass through the waters, I will be with you, and through the rivers, they will not overwhelm you. When you walk through the fire, you will not be burned or scorched, nor will the flame kindle upon you.

There are different ways to make pottery, depending on the type of clay, the different regions of the world, etc different techniques are used. However the most basic form is to first find the clay, work the clay out to remove any air bubbles that may cause it to explode later on while in the kiln, then to put the clay on the wheel or work it by hand, then glaze it with your chosen color, and then finally put it in the fire. If it all works out and no air bubbles are in the clay then viola you have a work of art. If you were a piece of pottery what kind would you be? What colors would you be adorned with? How valuable would you be?

It's no coincidence that Isaiah compared God to a potter. If you truly allow yourself to be worked on, He will. Not only will He work on you, but also He will make you a work of art for all to see. God loves to show off His work!

You may ask why would anyone want to be voluntarily put through the fire? Well it appears that this is not for everyone. If you know people who are the same way and stuck in their ways for years then you know exactly what I mean. However many have an innate need to find peace, to find a purpose, and to find themselves.

A finished piece of pottery can be worth millions depending on who put their hands on it to make it. So if God puts His hands on your spirit and begins to refine you like pure gold, how much more valuable will you be?

A true born again Christian can almost detect in what phase they are in, if they are being put through the fire or if they are going through the purifying phase, either way He won't leave you nor allow you to get burned. He is very quick to warn you, to soothe you, and to heal you while you are going through any of the phase. His main interest is not to scare you off but to draw you in, to make you whole, to make you a better person that goes from glory to glory and from victory to victory.

Today, think about your milestones. Can you remember when you were like raw Earth? Can you see how He has changed you? What were your milestones were you knew that it had to be God working in you?

Pray For You:
Father in the name of Jesus, Lord I pray that you continue to work in us, that you continue to refine us all on our own level and understanding. Lord have mercy on those that are used to provoke us, sometimes we miss the fact that you use others to test ourselves and to help in the refining process. I

Rosie Soroka M.S.

declare that we are all in your hands and that you know our past, our present, and our future; and all the work invested in all of us will give fruit 100% according to our calling. Lord thank you for investing in us: Your Son, Your Holy Spirit, Your love, Your time, Your angels, Your wisdom and gifts. We truly are a work of art in Your hands. In Jesus name. Amen.

~24~

Psalm 24

A Psalm of David.

1 THE EARTH is the Lord's, and the fullness of it, the world and they who dwell in it.

2 For He has founded it upon the seas and established it upon the currents and the rivers.

3 Who shall go up into the mountain of the Lord? Or who shall stand in His Holy Place?

4 He who has clean hands and a pure heart, who has not lifted himself up to falsehood or to what is false, nor sworn deceitfully.

5 He shall receive blessing from the Lord and righteousness from the God of his salvation.

6 This is the generation [description] of those who seek Him [who inquire of and for Him and of necessity require Him], who seek Your face, [O God of] Jacob. Selah [pause, and think of that]!

7 Lift up your heads, O you gates; and be lifted up, you age-abiding doors, that the King of glory may come in.

8 Who is the King of glory? The Lord strong and mighty, the Lord mighty in battle.

9 Lift up your heads, O you gates; yes, lift them up, you age-abiding doors, that the King of glory may come in.

10 Who is [He then] this King of glory? The Lord of hosts, He is the King of glory. Selah [pause, and think of that]!

Open your doors!

Today reflect on who is the Great I Am, and open the doors to your spirit and let Him in.

~MOTHER~

Exodus 20:12 (New King James Version): 12 " Honor your father and your mother, that your days may be long upon the land which the LORD your God is giving you.

Dearest Mother,

I would love to tell you publicly how I feel about you. It is my privilege to honor you on this very special day. You are truly a Proverbs 31 women. You are a special star in the sky that shines so bright, your rays are seen for miles abroad. Your smile lights up any person's fallen spirit. You have been the one that has awakened at all hours in the morning to pray for all of us. I believe that your prayers have kept me alive throughout my wild days, and I know that they were the cause for my change. Thank you for interceding for me, thank you for always listening to me and giving me wise advise. You have been there for me when I have been alone, you have always been available when I just needed a friend. Your youthful spirit is my joy. The happiness that radiates from you has always been a true blessing for all of us. You have been an example of a loving mother full of beauty and grace. You have gently covered our pains and covered our faults. You are never quick to shout nor uncover our weakness to others. Your loving hand has always been there to say "Sana Sana."

You are a beautiful rose that beguiles others with your sweet scent of love. Your compassion for others is truly genuine and sincere. Thank you for understanding your position in Christ, and for positioning yourself in the front lines like a true prayer warrior to fight for your family. On this day I want to tell you that I love you and God Bless YOU!!!

Today, take the time to honor your mother according to the Word of God. Remember the Bible does not say honor your parents if..... It is a spiritual law, and this is the first Commandment that carries a promise with it. So express something different to your mother in this day.

Prayer For All The Mothers:

Lord I pray that on this very special day Lord that your mercy and grace covers and shines on all the mothers all over the world. I pray that you put in the hearts of those around each one of them to honor them according to their works. Lord I pray that You fill each mother around the world with patience, strength, with the courage to continue fighting the good fight, and with the grace to love freely. Father I pray in the name of Jesus that You cover them all with Your mighty hand. In the name of Jesus. Amen.

~HIPPOPOTAMUS~

2 Corinthians 12:19-20 (New Living Translation): 19 Perhaps you think we're saying these things just to defend ourselves. No, we tell you this as Christ's servants, and with God as our witness. Everything we do, dear friends, is to strengthen you. **20** For I am afraid that when I come I won't like what I find, and you won't like my response. I am afraid that I will find quarreling, jealousy, anger, selfishness, slander, gossip, arrogance, and disorderly behavior.

Proverbs 25:21(Amplified Bible): 21 If your enemy is hungry, give him bread to eat; and if he is thirsty, give him water to drink;

Hippopotamus's are one of the most aggressive animals alive. In Africa they account for more human deaths than any other animal. In other words they are more dangerous than crocodiles, lions, and snakes. If hippos were humans they probably wouldn't be Christians.

One of the most amazing things about hippos is their skin. The skin itself is practically hairless and somewhat delicate and sensitive to the harsh African sun. When the hippo is outside of the water the skin oozes a pinkish liquid that is used like a sun-block so the skin doesn't burn. Hippo skin also has a very thick layer of fat that protects them from the harsh weather and hostile environments.

Hippo skin although illegal to have in the physical form, very much recommended having in the spiritual form. As we see in 2 Corinthians 12:19-20, we can expect at some point being the target of gossip, jealousy, anger, etc. Then at some point you can expect God to test your heart, or maybe even show a lesson to the gossiper through your kindness. Regardless, everything slides off hippo skin, mud, water, and it even creates its own sun-block. Our sun-block is our intimacy with God; a moment in His presence allows us to recharge and move on in our daily walk, while truly forgiving those that have trespassed against us.

Today think back to those people that have hurt you and picture a nice fat layer of hippo skin on your skin, like a full body suit. Next imagine what they said or whatever actions they did was water, now picture that water rolling right off of you. Lastly say out loud, "I love my new hippo skin, everything rolls right off it." Now in the future when you find yourself being attacked just picture that hippo skin right on you, and give thanks to God for your new skin.

~In?~

Proverbs 6:30-31 (New Living Translation): 30 Excuses might be found for a thief who steals because he is starving. 31 But if he is caught, he must pay back seven times what he stole, even if he has to sell everything in his house.

1 Peter 5:8-9 (Amplified Bible): 8 Be well balanced (temperate, sober of mind), be vigilant and cautious at all times; for that enemy of yours, the devil, roams around like a lion roaring [in fierce hunger], seeking someone to seize upon and devour.

John 10:10 (Amplified Bible): 10 The thief comes only in order to steal and kill and destroy. I came that they may have and enjoy life, and have it in abundance (to the full, till it overflows).

**Don't be a duck, take your position in the
battle next to Jesus!**

A prestigious man once went to a beautiful country were many recognized artists and some of the most creative thinkers originated from. The prime minister was very pleased to receive him and invited him to the best restaurant in town for lunch. As they pulled up with their security escort to the restaurant, the young man looked around and was somewhat shocked at the conditions of the city. The restaurant itself would be equivalent to a hole in the wall here. The food was served, and it seemed anything but appetizing. The young man shocked and disappointed at the incongruent stories he had heard about the majestic city, asked the prime minister, "What do you supposed happened to the city in the span of 30 years that made such an impact on the society?" The prime minister a little bit embarrassed and very much interested in maintaining appearances began philosophizing on different possibilities.

One of the armed guards face began to show his annoyance with the conversation. The young man asked the guard, "What do you think?" The guard said, "Let me show you what I think." He asked the waitress for a duck, a live duck. The waitress looked at the eyes of the party she was attending and noticed that everyone was serious, so she went to the back and brought back a live duck. The guard then took the duck out of her hands and began to pull out the ducks feathers handfuls at a time. As the duck cried out, while everyone in the restaurant froze in shock.

When the majority of the feathers were ripped out the duck was then thrown on the floor. The duck laid in small pools of blood shivering and limping about. The soldier then asked the waitress to bring some bread, and she did. The guard then put the bread in his hand and the duck began to limp over to him and began to eat it right out of his hand. The guard looked up and said, "If you torture and break down the peoples spirit then give them food, even if its a little bit, they will follow you even if it kills them."

Oppression comes in many forms, not just the physical form, but also an emotional and spiritual form. Like this story many people are the duck. Many times people are barely getting by emotionally, spiritually, or physically but they keep on doing the same things that got them their in the first place. For example a couple on the verge of divorcing because they don't spend enough time together, they continuously work and chase after their paycheck; as if that will rub their backs when they need encouragement or say, "I love you." Another example may be a child that may be in the verge of using drugs or running away while the parents go chasing after their own delights, trying to live "their" life; then they wonder why the child hates themselves or hates them. The news is full of examples, some of the more disturbing ones are of how mothers kill their newborn babies because they wanted to date someone who didn't want a baby. There are so many examples that can be expressed that could go on for days, it's all around us.

If circumstances move you to act in an ungodly way, then you are a duck and your feathers may not have all been plucked out all at once, but maybe a feather at a time over a period of time. The feather plucking can be characterized as a failed relationship, rebellious children, struggling to find or keep a job, being alone, having made bad decisions in the past and living with regret, feeling unloved and not appreciated, being full of bitterness, just to describe a few.

If this is the case, there is a way to get your feathers back. According to the Bible, what the enemy has stolen from you, each blessing, every tear cried out of pain, needs to be returned back to you seven times over. If you believe that then you are entitle to restitution.

Today, think back to the blessings that you know came from God that you know were taken from you, whether it was a marriage, an in-converse spouse, a disobedient child, your finances, your hope, whatever it is and begin to declare the Word of God over them.

Pray Out-Loud:
Father, I give you thanks for all the many blessings You have given me and trusted me with. I pray that you forgive me for not fighting the way that I was supposed to fight to keep them, but today in the name of Jesus and with the authority given to me by You, I declare Your Word over the blessings stolen by the enemy. (Point your finger at the

ground and begin to say out-loud). I declare in the name of Jesus that you have been discovered and you must return to me each of my blessings that you took from me sevenfold, according to the Word of God. In the name of Jesus return them to me now: my joy, my family, my ministry, (whatever it is you need to declare it out-loud). In the name of Jesus. Amen.

~Model~

Revelation 5:5 (King James Version): 5 And one of the elders saith unto me, Weep not: behold, the Lion of the tribe of Judah, the Root of David, hath prevailed to open the book, and to loose the seven seals thereof.

Genesis 49:9 (New Living Translation): 9 Judah, my son, is a young lion that has finished eating its prey. Like a lion he crouches and lies down; like a lioness—who dares to rouse him?

2 Timothy 1:4-6 (Amplified Bible): 4 and when, as I recall your tears, I yearn to see you so that I may be filled with joy. **5** I am calling up memories of your sincere and unqualified faith (the leaning of your entire personality on God in Christ in absolute trust and confidence in His power, wisdom, and goodness), [a faith] that first lived permanently in [the heart of] your grandmother Lois and your mother Eunice and now, I am [fully] persuaded, [dwells] in you also. **6** That is why I would remind you to stir up (rekindle the embers of, fan the flame of, and keep burning) the [gracious] gift of God, [the inner fire] that is in you by means of the laying on of my hands [with those of the elders at your ordination].

Are you a Jesus cub that chases away the enemy?

When the king of the jungle roars, it can be heard for up to five miles away. Everything in its direct path is shaken and awaken. The cubs from when they are small they practice roaring and playing. As they get older the things they copy become more intense and more life threatening. They must learn how to hunt and fend for themselves, they must learn how to defend their pride and how to survive in hostile environments.

If our role model is, as adults, Jesus, then who is the role model of our children? The answer is us. By demonstrating to children the love of God we are creating an environment of forgiveness and acceptance. By demonstrating faith to our children we are creating an environment of hope, strength and endurance. By demonstrating prayer and worship we are demonstrating power and wisdom. What is the example that you are demonstrating? If your children were lion cubs would they roar loudly, softly, or run in fear?

Timothy was a timid young man that grew up in a home were his mother was left a widow early on in his life. However, his mother was a prayer warrior and her mother was a prayer warrior. Their faith established and affirmed Timothy at a very early age. Oddly enough children get it, sometimes faster and more in-depth than adults; and he got it and understood when the Apostle Paul said to him what he said in the Biblical verse. He understood that in his bloodline was that determined faith and boldness to reach his calling because his mother and her mother had that faith and modeled it in their home were he grew up. Timothy later grew up and went from a shy and timid young man to an Apostle of Jesus working and ministering to the multitudes with power and boldness.

Today ask for the revelation of what it means to be a cub of the Lion. Can your roar be heard five miles away or more? Can the enemy hear your roar? Ask your children, "What's going on in your spiritual lives?" Ask if they feel alone, unappreciated, or unloved, sometimes children and teens find it difficult to verbalize what they feel so ask. Ask yourself, "What kind of role model am I?" Are you showing your children to roar? Are you showing them to defend what is theirs? Are you planting the seeds of faith? Keep in mind that this goes further than just attending church on Sundays.

~CAVE~

Isaiah 40:29 (Amplified Bible): 29 He gives power to the faint and weary, and to him who has no might He increases strength [causing it to multiply and making it to abound].

2 Samuel 23:8 (New Living Translation): David's Mightiest Warriors: 8 These are the names of David's mightiest warriors. The first was Jashobeam the Hacmonite, who was leader of the Three—the three mightiest warriors among David's men. He once used his spear to kill 800 enemy warriors in a single battle.

2 Samuel 21:19-30 (Amplified Bible): 19 There was again war at Gob with the Philistines, and Elhanan son of Jaare-oregim, a Bethlehemite, slew Goliath the Gittite, whose spear shaft was like a weaver's beam. 20 And there was again war at Gath, where there was a man of great stature who had six fingers on each hand and six toes on each foot, twenty-four in number; he also was a descendant of the giants. 21 And when he defied Israel, Jonathan son of Shimei, brother of David, slew him. 22 These four were descended from the giant in Gath, and they fell by the hands of David and his servants.

**Sometimes the cave is more precious than
it looks from the outside.**

Many animals seek refuge during the winter days in caves and many hibernate for months at a time until the spring. During the springtime new life comes out of the caves, many baby animals spring out ready to explore their new environments, and others just wake up with new fur.

Our soul is the same way. We need to hibernate sometimes and gather new strengths to move into another spiritual level. Sometimes its difficult for us to accept the "cave" phase because it seems as though something was taken away, perhaps you and your spouse are divorcing, or you lost your job, or you lost a friendship, or a business; but God can easily bring you peace and an increase in all those areas in a flash. The point is to take advantage of the hiatus and get closer to God. In the cave you will find refuge, a fresh encounter with God, and so much more. Were you are weak, He will give you new strengths, were you lack He will fulfill. Perhaps you need nothing, but He can give you passion for others and make you feel again. Whatever the reason you find yourself in the cave trust that God put you there for a good reason and for your own growth.

When David killed Goliath the giant, he was very young, when Saul hunted David he found refuge in caves all along the coasts and borders. David wrote the sweetest Psalms under these conditions, death was waiting for him at every corner yet he found refuge.

People in similar conditions, in debt, escaped slaves, outlaws, and such banned together with him and he put them all in the cave. While in the cave the men received strength, leadership, and a fresh encounter with God. When they came out of the cave they were all known as David's Men of Valor and recognized for their courage throughout Israel. During the various battles David's men actually killed many more giants than he did, and when David was made king those Men of Valor rose to the top with him. Which brings up another quality David had that made him such an effective leader, he was neither intimidated nor jealous of his men. David also celebrated their victories as if they were his own. His actions were the exact opposite of Saul's, when the cities cried out songs of joy saying, "Saul killed a thousand and David killed ten thousand," Saul was filled with insecurities, jealousy, and wanted David dead.

Today, think back to a time when you were in the cave or if you are currently in there think about, how did or will you come out? What did you learn? What is/was your attitude? If currently you find yourself in a cave, don't worry, Gods doing it for your own growth. You will leave the cave stronger and what was loss will be replenished and multiplied according to your measure of faith.

~13~

Psalm 13 (Amplified Bible)

Psalm 13

To the Chief Musician. A Psalm of David.

1 HOW LONG will You forget me, O Lord? Forever? How long will You hide Your face from me?

2 How long must I lay up cares within me and have sorrow in my heart day after day? How long shall my enemy exalt himself over me?

3 Consider and answer me, O Lord my God; lighten the eyes [of my faith to behold Your face in the pitchlike darkness], lest I sleep the sleep of death,

4 Lest my enemy say, I have prevailed over him, and those that trouble me rejoice when I am shaken.

5 But I have trusted, leaned on, and been confident in Your mercy and loving-kindness; my heart shall rejoice and be in high spirits in Your salvation.

6 I will sing to the Lord, because He has dealt bountifully with me

"My eyes are on You, my God!"

Rosie Soroka M.S.

Today, reflect on your attitude towards Gods presence. Is this relationship essential to you? Do you trust Him? Can you sing while your going through the storm? Learn to trust Him the same way that David did and be blessed, and bless your following generations.

~Bear~

Genesis 2:1-3 (New Living Translation): 1 So the creation of the heavens and the earth and everything in them was completed. 2 On the seventh day God had finished his work of creation, so he rested from all his work. 3 And God blessed the seventh day and declared it holy, because it was the day when he rested from all his work of creation.

Exodus 23:12 (New Living Translation): 12 "You have six days each week for your ordinary work, but on the seventh day you must stop working. This gives your ox and your donkey a chance to rest. It also allows your slaves and the foreigners living among you to be refreshed.

Hebrews 4:10 (New Living Translation): 10 For all who have entered into God's rest have rested from their labors, just as God did after creating the world.

Your body has been equipped with what is known as the 'flight or fight' response to stress/threat. Briefly, what this means is that if a bear jumped right in front of you about to attack you, your body will shut down certain non-essential things immediately to use all your energy to either run or fight. A jolt of Adrenaline is released into your bloodstream, your stomach stops digesting, your pupils open up to see better in the dark, your energy is shifted into you muscles, and you are instantly awakened. This was designed as a survival tool, however one is not meant to live constantly in that state, your body can't take that type of pressure well for long periods of time.

Throughout the years stress has been discovered to be somewhat like a ninja, you never know were in your body it will attack, nor do you know were it came from. On a daily basis we are all affected by different levels of stress. Everybody has a different bear that may be charging after them, maybe from work, bills, a doctor's diagnosis, children, school, a mother-in- law, or whatever else. Living under the constant gun of stress has been linked to heart disease, high blood pressure, stroke, cancer, and other health problems. Maybe you rationalize your current stress level, but your health report may differ with what your opinion is.

God designed our bodies and made us in His image. He also required that the seventh day (whatever day your congregation determines), whether Saturday or Sunday, one day is to rest. You need to rest your body, mind, and spirit. There is enough going on all the time were you really can take a day out just to rest and give God thanks.

Perhaps your schedule looks so packed that you may think you cannot take the time off, but whatever time you take even if its just to rest, God will return it back to you. "How?" Well in many forms, perhaps the time you didn't stress out increased your years of life, maybe God cut your expected line waiting time at the post office in half so you wouldn't be there for so long. God is a creative God and has many ways to redeem our time.

Today, think about what your bear is that causes you stress. Whatever it is you can deal with it six days out of the week, on the seventh day rest.

(If it's your kids that cause you stress then just enjoy them, plan out a special day with them and have fun. They grow up quickly).

~ENCOURAGED~

Proverbs 17:17 (New Living Translation: 17 A friend is always loyal, and a brother is born to help in time of need.

Proverbs 12:25 (Amplified Bible): 25 Anxiety in a man's heart weighs it down, but an encouraging word makes it glad.

Proverbs 15:13 (Amplified Bible): 13 A glad heart makes a cheerful countenance, but by sorrow of heart the spirit is broken.

If you ever waited in a line and observed the people around you and saw their faces, you would be able to get a good idea of what they are thinking about. Perhaps the anxiety of expecting the grocery bill to be to high, or the frowns because they have been waiting for what seems like forever; it can be anything. Even though we may be inclined to think we know what they are thinking, we may or may not be right, we don't really know them. The people we do know very well, we can very quickly pick up on their feelings and thoughts. You are more in-tuned with that person because of your history with them and your relationship with them.

Sometimes inadvertently we lend ourselves to make our friends feel worse about a situation or a person and we fail to take that as an opportunity to give a good word of encouragement or a good word of exhortation.

God has given us all amazing gifts, but one gift we all can have is to encourage one another. A simple smile and a big fat hug can really make someone's day. A few words of just saying, "Hey you're doing a great job," can truly cheer someone up. We are not designed to be alone nor to take on the burdens of the world by ourselves as if we were the Almighty Himself. No. We are designed to give to others and receive from others. Today your brother, sister, or a stranger needs a word of encouragement, will you give it to them?

Today, sow in Gods Kingdom, open your mouth to declare a blessing over someone, open your mouth and give a word of consolation, acceptance, love, and encouragement. Do not keep it to yourself, express it and be free; free to love others; free to caress someone's soul; free to express feelings. Don't expect anything back, and begin feeling the love that you have inside shine out!

Prayer For You:
Father in the name of Jesus, Lord I pray that you put a person in need of an encouraging word in front of all those people willing to speak a word of hope into their lives. Father let Your children have a revelation of what it is to sow these words of life to others; and show them how a few words can change a persons outlook and even perspective on things. Guard our mouths Lord from becoming stumbling blocks for others, guard our mouths Father from taking someone else's peace. Lord guard our mouths from cursing other peoples lives. Father give us all Your eyes to see others with compassion and love that You see us with. In Jesus name. Amen.

~LOVED~

Romans 8:35-36 (Amplified Bible): 35 Who shall ever separate us from Christ's love? Shall suffering and affliction and tribulation? Or calamity and distress? Or persecution or hunger or destitution or peril or sword?

Often times Christianity is refereed to as a religion, but is that really what it is? The word religion can be used as a noun or as an adjective, however someone who has had revelation of whom Jesus is and what this means in their lives would more likely refer to Christianity as a verb. Love is many things and you have to work at it, you have to show it and you have to mean it. Why is it so important to love? Because it is part of our design. Love is necessary in our daily life, it is also an essential part of our soul. Without it we are not whole.

If you have had a revelation of what Jesus love is like then the Living Word of God which is the Bible becomes real to you and living. This verse stands true, what could ever separate us from Jesus? No trial, storm, tribulation can. Only you can. Unfortunately if you chose to be separated then you are... only until you go back. When you do, you can expect to be welcomed back with open arms and an overabundance of love.

Today, just know that you are loved. Someone made you for a purpose and will direct your steps to a better life, to better people, and to amazing blessings if you allow Him to.

Prayer For You:

In the name of Jesus, Father, I establish from the heavens to the Earth, from the invisible to the visible, each and everyone of your children's plan and purpose. I declare that each one of Your children will begin to walk in their calling, in their purpose on this Earth to bring You all the glory. I declare that our future generations walk face to face with You, hand in hand with You. I declare that Your Words and Spirit are lamps at their feet guiding them in every decision. From now, I pray in Jesus name, that you separate from each one of their paths, those that will harm them or attempt to separate them from You. In Jesus name. Amen.

~BONES~

Ezekiel 37:3-13 (New Living Translation): 3 Then he asked me, "Son of man, can these bones become living people again?" "O Sovereign Lord," I replied, "you alone know the answer to that." **4** Then he said to me, "Speak a prophetic message to these bones and say, 'Dry bones, listen to the word of the Lord! **5** This is what the Sovereign Lord says: Look! I am going to put breath into you and make you live again! **6** I will put flesh and muscles on you and cover you with skin. I will put breath into you, and you will come to life. Then you will know that I am the Lord.'" **7** So I spoke this message, just as he told me. Suddenly as I spoke, there was a rattling noise all across the valley. The bones of each body came together and attached themselves as complete skeletons. **8** Then as I watched, muscles and flesh formed over the bones. Then skin formed to cover their bodies, but they still had no breath in them. **9** Then he said to me, "Speak a prophetic message to the winds, son of man. Speak a prophetic message and say, 'This is what the Sovereign Lord says: Come, O breath, from the four winds! Breathe into these dead bodies so they may live again.'" **10** So I spoke the message as he commanded me, and breath came into their bodies. They all came to life and stood up on their feet—a great army. **11** Then he said to me, "Son of man, these bones represent the people of Israel. They are saying, 'We have become old, dry bones—all hope is gone.

Our nation is finished.' **12** Therefore, prophesy to them and say, 'This is what the Sovereign Lord says: O my people, I will open your graves of exile and cause you to rise again. Then I will bring you back to the land of Israel. **13** When this happens, O my people, you will know that I am the Lord.

Do your bones have life?

If you have ever felt like an area in your life is as dry as a desert or as lifeless as a bone then this is the day to speak and prophesi over that area. No longer will you see that area as a bag of dead bones, but as an opportunity for God to show you that He is the Lord. Speak over that issue, that problem, those bones and continue to declare and prophesi over them.

Today, have faith, and believe that God can bring those areas back to life, just prophesi just like Ezekiel did.

~Grace~

Psalm 5:12 (King James Version): 12 For thou, LORD, wilt bless the righteous; with favor wilt thou compass him as with a shield.

Psalm 84:11 (King James Version): 11 For the Lord God is a Sun and Shield; the Lord bestows [present] grace and favor and [future] glory (honor, splendor, and heavenly bliss)! No good thing will He withhold from those who walk uprightly.

Ezra 9:8: And now, for a brief moment, grace has been shown us by the Lord our God, Who has left us a remnant to escape and has given us a secure hold in His holy place, that our God may brighten our eyes and give us a little reviving in our bondage.

Esther 2:17: And the king loved Esther more than all the women, and she obtained grace and favor in his sight more than all the maidens, so that he set the royal crown on her head and made her queen instead of Vashti.

A wise man once asked, "Would you rather a million dollars in your bank account or Gods grace and favor over you?" What would answer? Many would answer a million dollars, something you can see over something you can't see with your natural eyes, but before you answer the question lets expand a bit on this grace and favor thing. Have you ever seen someone that was simply irresistible, someone that if they asked for anything you would give it to them, even if you see them for the first time? Maybe a child, maybe a teenager, an adult, or even an elder. When you see them, there is something totally different about them and you somehow become beguiled by them. There is different areas that God puts grace and favor over someone, sometimes God puts favor over a future friend and all of a sudden you feel like you have known them forever, God is using grace and favor to accelerate that friendship. God does this all the time, amongst leaders, families, blended families, relationships, at work, and any other type of relationship.

When someone has grace and favor the room simply shines when that person enters. Grace and favor can catapult you to limitless levels of influence, fidelity, it can open doors that you never even thought possible. These two powerful blessings from God can penetrate any area of anything even were money cannot.

There have been countless stories of soldiers and refugee's alike that have been spared by Gods favor and grace. Stories of economic hardships all around, yet some manage to pull overtime, keep a job, get hired, or even get promoted. Look at Esther and just contemplate how she went from an orphan to the Queen of the whole entire Persian Empire, how? Grace and favor. King David was also well aware of what grace and favor meant and what it could do, that's why he constantly praised God for giving him those things.

On the flip side of not having grace and favor, are the stories of those who have the millions and are forbidden to leave anywhere because they are wanted all over the world for crimes or injustices. Millionaires who not even their families can stand to be around and are lonely. People who have what we think may be everything, and end up killing themselves because they were always rejected or just completely unhappy. This is not the case for every single well off person, nor should a person have a mentality that God only loves the poor, He loves all the same, however it is food for thought. Were can grace and favor take you?

Today, strive for what God has placed in your heart and pray for that grace and favor that will launch you to new heights and declare it over your generations as well.

~1~

Psalm 1 (King James Version)

1 Blessed is the man that walketh not in the counsel of the ungodly, nor standeth in the way of sinners, nor sitteth in the seat of the scornful. **2** But his delight is in the law of the LORD; and in his law doth he meditate day and night. **3** And he shall be like a tree planted by the rivers of water, that bringeth forth his fruit in his season; his leaf also shall not wither; and whatsoever he doeth shall prosper. **4** The ungodly are not so: but are like the chaff which the wind driveth away. **5** Therefore the ungodly shall not stand in the judgment, nor sinners in the congregation of the righteous. **6** For the LORD knoweth the way of the righteous: but the way of the ungodly shall perish.

Plant yourself in Jesus and give fruit in your season!

Today just meditate on His Words, continue to declare it over your life, and be fruitful.

~Dollar~

Exodus 19:4-5 (Amplified Bible): 4 You have seen what I did to the Egyptians, and how I bore you on eagles' wings and brought you to Myself. 5 Now therefore, if you will obey My voice in truth and keep My covenant, then you shall be My own peculiar possession and treasure from among and above all peoples; for all the earth is Mine.

What areas in your life need be ironed out?

If you had a hundred dollar bill in your hand fresh from the bank we would agree that that dollar would be worth a hundred ones, or ten 10 dollar bills, or five twenty dollar bills. That hundred dollars even if it was completely wrinkled it would still be worth that hundred dollars, even if it had coffee stains or any other stains it would still be worth that amount, right? Imagine a hundred dollar bill found on the sidewalk of a city, all dirty and wrinkled, if you found it would you keep it or throw it away?

You are that hundred dollar bill, picture that each wrinkle and each stain was some trauma, drama, curse, rejection, a really bad moment or whatever you may have gone through that was hard. The wrinkles can also represent areas in your personality that are making you unhappy, making others unhappy; or areas that are damaging to you or others. You see the enemy knows your worth and since before you were born the enemy has been working to establish folds and tears in you through rejections, failures, etc. Now imagine the enemy folding you, crushing you, stepping on you, and every so often he gives you a break so you can feel as though you may have some glimpse of hope; and then all of a sudden 'BAM' back to the floor under his foot, again to smash your dreams, your desires, your hopes, and your identity.

Through time you may build resentment towards others, hatred, low self esteem, lack of forgiveness, you may look at your circumstances and not be able to see God.

Now imagine you fell into Jesus hands, and from the moment on you allow Him to begin working on you. Now picture Him looking at you and with His hands He begins to open one of the folded areas. That area may be really hard and painful for you to open, it may require that you forgive a person that abused you or hurt you, but with His patience and love you work on it, and you succeed. Then all of a sudden another wrinkled has to get ironed out and it is something else, maybe your pride, or ego, or another failed relationship, whatever it is it hurts...again. Now depending on your openness to Him, the wrinkles and the stains start coming off of you. Slowly you begin to take form and you start looking like a hundred dollar bill... again.

Before you know it, you begin to see yourself and you begin to remember the condition that Jesus found you in and then you see how the hands of God changed you, and its amazing. Soon you don't even recognize that old person that you were; that person that was unhappy, miserable, jealous, and short tempered has left the building and what is left is a person that God has deemed as valuable and as a treasure.

Today, allow Jesus in your heart, allow Him to smooth out each and every one of your wrinkles, allow Him to heal your past traumas, allow Him to change those areas in your personality that impede you from having a happy and fulfilling life. In Jesus name. Amen.

~Pedicure~

Romans 10:14-15 (New International Version): 14 How, then, can they call on the one they have not believed in? And how can they believe in the one of whom they have not heard? **15** And how can they hear without someone preaching to them? And how can anyone preach unless they are sent? As it is written: "How beautiful are the feet of those who bring good news!"

Are your feet beautiful according to God?

Shoe industries worldwide make billions of dollars yearly selling shoes. Some designers even use real gold and precious diamonds to decorate them, the price range on those shoes could even be in the millions. Many movie stars and musicians are faithful customers to these designers and strut their stuff as they walk down the red carpet or other award shows.

If you were in a desert and were dehydrated about to die and all of a sudden collapse with no hope of surviving, would you accept a cup of water from someone with designer shoes, dirty sandals, or it just wouldn't even matter?

In many cases when a persons survival is threatened it wouldn't really matter what kind of shoes they had on or how unfiltered the water was, most of us would accept the water and be most grateful.

You would be surprised how many people are walking in a spiritual desert, walking about on the verge of collapsing or throwing in the towel. Some of the most famous words people say when they find out that a person committed suicide or just snapped is "I never would have guessed..." We are not here to assume or to guess, we are here to testify. God has touched every persons life whether they know it or not, He leaves seeds behind and when someone testifies, that person may begin to think, "Hmmm, God did something like that for me." Then slowly those seeds begin to grow into small plants of faith, because through testimonies from others, people begin to make connections in their own lives. Before you know it someone you testified to begins to testify to others as well.

Beautiful, truly are the feet of those that bring the water to those in the desert, both physically and spiritually, and Jesus calls us to do both. You can testify to friends, family, strangers, but the most important people to share your testimonies are with your children. Their faith is amazing, you may be surprised when they begin to testify to you or give you words of encouragement.

Today open your mouth and give thanks to God by testifying to someone, tell them what God has done for you and how He can do it for them; you just may be bringing water to a thirsty soul.

~Foxes~

Judges 15:4-5 (Amplified Bible): 4 So Samson went and caught 300 foxes or jackals and took torches and turning the foxes tail to tail, he put a torch between each pair of tails. **5** And when he had set the torches ablaze, he let the foxes go into the standing grain of the Philistines, and he burned up the shocks and the standing grain, along with the olive orchards.

Song of Solomon 2:15 (King James Version): 15 Take us the foxes, the little foxes, that spoil the vines: for our vines have tender grapes.

Foxholes are the beginning of a lost cause.

When a relationship begins to go bad it usually started by small things. The way that person talked to you that one time, or that person did something or does something that makes you upset. The things that don't get spoken about or the small things that add up are foxes, for example, maybe it's a disrespectful gesture, or a name someone called you. These things are like foxes that come and tear out little bites out of a tender relationship. God's Word talks to us about being careful with these types of actions, because in the long run they spoil your joy and relationships.

97

For close friends it may take several foxes before a relationship is torn down, however for newly made friends it may take very little. Truth is everyone is going to get offended every once in a while, so before you talk about it, pray about it. Ask God to filter your words and open each other's hearts so you can say what's going on without offending the other person or starting an argument. You cannot control someone else's actions, however you can control your own; so take control of your foxes; and when someone else's foxes come to get you, catch them and talk about it at the right moment. (Notice, the right moment doesn't mean it has to be that very minute, take time to cool down first).

Today, ask God to reveal to you what are some areas in your life that have been ravaged by foxes and ask God for direction. Also ask Him if you're the owner of a fox that is a pestilence to someone else and ask Him how you can eliminate that nuisance.

~Cursed~

Matthew 27:24-26 (Amplified Bible): 24 So when Pilate saw that he was getting nowhere, but rather that a riot was about to break out, he took water and washed his hands in the presence of the crowd, saying, I am not guilty of nor responsible for this righteous Man's blood; see to it yourselves. **25** And all the people answered, Let His blood be on us and on our children! **26** So he set free for them Barabbas; and he [had] Jesus whipped, and delivered Him up to be crucified.

Matthew 16:19 (King James Version): 19 And I will give unto thee the keys of the kingdom of heaven: and whatsoever thou shalt bind on earth shall be bound in heaven: and whatsoever thou shalt loose on earth shall be loosed in heaven.

Reading this verse and understanding the power of words you can imagine how God must have felt at the moment the people said this. He must have tried to cover His ears to not hear how His children cursed themselves. What pain it must be to see your children go down a path that is complete opposite of your hearts desire. Perhaps in these days now, people no longer say things like, "Let his blood be on me and my children," however many people continue to curse their children and their family.

Countless of times the word 'damned' or 'cursed' are used in daily language. In fact parents, teachers, and others in authoritative positions use these words to describe children, teenagers, and adults all the time.

These words are more than words they are orders that are being established like a blessing, only difference is that the God is not the one being invoked, its the enemy.

Today be very aware of what you say or what others are saying around you; and if someone uses those words against you or your family cancel it in Jesus name.

Prayer for you:

Lord in the name of Jesus, Father I pray that you cover all Your children with the blood of Christ. Father I declare that no weapon forged against them shall prosper. I declare that any words spoken against them that are designed to curse them or make them captives are canceled and fall at their feet, in Jesus name. Amen.

~SALMON~

Philippians 3:13-14 (Amplified Bible): 13 I do not consider, brethren, that I have captured and made it my own [yet]; but one thing I do [it is my one aspiration]: forgetting what lies behind and straining forward to what lies ahead, **14** I press on toward the goal to win the [supreme and heavenly] prize to which God in Christ Jesus is calling us upward.

Every year Salmon make a journey commonly known as the Salmon Run. This is when Salmon swim back up to the rivers were they were born from to lay their own eggs. It is a difficult struggle for each individual fish, between the sport fishermen, the bears, the sharp-edged rocks that cut through their skin, and the regular fishermen it's a wonder how these Salmon continue to breed. If you were a Salmon and knew that the road ahead of you was going to be difficult, would you just give up and let the first bear eat you? Or would you continue pressing through in hopes of the prize?

Even though most of their trip back to there birthing grounds is upstream and dangerous they continue. Funny enough we can learn from these fish many things like: persistence, endurance, motivation, stamina, determination, and perseverance. All that from a Salmon.

It is shocking to see how many people from all walks of life and all social statuses walk about life carrying on to past pains. Those that naturally have a tendency to shake things off fast are incredibly blessed even if they don't know it. For those that are not naturally born with the ability to let the past go quickly, that is okay, we are all made differently. However, in order to move forward a person needs to get a permanent marker and draw a line separating the past from the future. Your past does not dictate you future, nor does your past make you who you are going to be.

Even though your beginnings may be humble your future is full of possibilities and hope. There is a God that has your best interest at heart, the real question here is, is He in your heart?

Today ask God to reveal to you the areas that are stopping you from moving forward, maybe a past mistake, a past relationship, past trauma, past abuse, bad parents, drugs, whatever it is God is telling you to LET IT GO! He has new and amazing things for you, but you have to give Him your pains, let go and forgive. You may be losing the chance of a lifetime because of your past!

~CAIMAN~

Isaiah 43:23 (Amplified Bible): 23 You have not brought Me your sheep and goats for burnt offerings, or honored Me with your sacrifices. I have not required you to serve with an offering or treated you as a slave by demanding tribute or wearied you with offering incense.

Malachi 3:10-11 (Amplified Bible): 10 Bring all the tithes (the whole tenth of your income) into the storehouse, that there may be food in My house, and prove Me now by it, says the Lord of hosts, if I will not open the windows of heaven for you and pour you out a blessing, that there shall not be room enough to receive it. **11** And I will rebuke the devourer [insects and plagues] for your sakes and he shall not destroy the fruits of your ground, neither shall your vine drop its fruit before the time in the field, says the Lord of hosts.

Caiman alligators mostly live in Central and South America, a very unique quality that these alligator's posses is that they can stand up on their back legs. When they do, the stubbiness of their front arms becomes very apparent and measure only a few inches. Imagine one of these Caiman's wearing pants, and maybe even a tee shirt. Would you go near it, or would you keep your distance regardless of the disguise? Could that Caiman reach in his or her pocket with those short stubby arms? Probably not. So not only is a

Caiman capable of standing on his or her two feet, but they can't reach their pockets to give, but it is also a reptile that people would run from instinctively. Do you know people who are synonyms with Caimans?

In the spiritual world people can perceive what kind of person you are. You can see it if you know what to look for. If we can see a little bit, (some may call intuition), what do you think God can see? Well, He can see the good, the bad, and the ugly (Caimans) hearts at all times. When you give, your heart automatically goes through an x-ray and you know exactly what goes through your mind at that time. It may be joy because you have had revelation of what offering can unleash in your life, or it may be that your offering God what is left over and with a mentality that is not a mentality appreciated by God. Malachi 3:10-11 is the only verse in the Bible were God says "prove me..." and in other versions He says "test Me..."

Today, well, test Him! Tithing and offerings are not forced on anyone, however they are your chance to get blessed financially. (*Hint, hint* Tithing is your 10% of your earnings, offerings are additional to tithing. Giving offerings is more like giving someone something they need, it doesn't necessarily have to be money, it can be like clothes, paying for someone's lunch, helping friends or family, whatever God puts in your heart and you do it with a good attitude.

Prayer For You:
Lord in the name of Jesus, Father I pray. Lord I pray that Your children have revelation to what an amazing experience it is to eat the fruit but return to you the seed so you can keep multiplying it. Thank you for showing us Your laws of sowing and reaping, and harvesting at the right time. In Jesus name I unleash Your Words over all of our finances and declare that You will prove Yourself more than capable to supply our every need because You are a living God that loves obedience in His children and never oversees our sacrifices, nor the heart that we give it with. In Jesus name. Amen.

~CAKE~

Genesis 2:8-9 (New Living Translation): **8** Then the Lord God planted a garden in Eden in the east, and there he placed the man he had made. **9** The Lord God made all sorts of trees grow up from the ground—trees that were beautiful and that produced delicious fruit. In the middle of the garden he placed the tree of life and the tree of the knowledge of good and evil.

Genesis 3:6 (New Living Translation): **6** The woman was convinced. She saw that the tree was beautiful and its fruit looked delicious, and she wanted the wisdom it would give her. So she took some of the fruit and ate it. Then she gave some to her husband, who was with her, and he ate it, too.

If someone cooked your favorite cake, with all the yummy frosting and trimmings, then cut you a slice and laid it in front of you what would be your thoughts? Would it be along the lines of, "YUMMY!" would you be salivating in anticipation of your first bite? Or would you be analyzing and thinking, "Well this cake looks like they used a cup of flour and two teaspoons of vanilla extract and well I have to taste it to see how many eggs it has..."

Now consider this, a yummy looking cake that provokes all your taste buds, but the second you put it in your mouth, its the nastiest thing you have ever had the displeasure to taste.

In the second example you believed with your eyes and what your senses said about the cake only to find out you were mislead. In first example you had a choice to either analyze the cakes ingredients or just enjoy it. So now the question is do your senses dictate what you believe?

You see when Eve and Adam ate from the tree of the knowledge of good and evil what they ate up was reasoning... Adam and Eve before that moment didn't know anything other than God, and Gods natural state is supernatural. In order for man to have access to that state again, God gave us faith. Through faith we can access Gods point of view and see what is not visible making it visible. The second you mix up your five senses and begin to reason you loose your miracle, you loose your revelation, and you miss out on Gods natural state. Reasoning is faiths worst enemy.

If your know some of the stories from the Bible you can definitely see that God is creative and has a sense of humor that is worthy of a chuckle. Look at Jonah, three days in a whale's stomach? Or Noah, building an ark without even knowing what rain was. Consider how God shut the animal's appetite so they wouldn't eat each other for 40 days. Or even more interesting how the animals from all over heard Gods voice and went for a walk to the ark, lined up and ready to go.

God is amazing, let Him do amazing things for you, let Him add adventure, let Him be the one that you trust in, let Him be the one that you look for in good times and in bad times. We are all vulnerable, some its through your finances, others its through your children, either way its better to look for God now so when the storms come your planted on solid ground.

Today, ask God for a revelation, and search for Him. Don't ever put God in four walls or ever put your human limitations on Him, think big and allow Him through faith to move on your behalf! In other words eat the cake and enjoy every single bite!

~IMMORTALITY~

Acts 28:4-6 (King James Version): 4 And when the barbarians saw the venomous beast hang on his hand, they said among themselves, No doubt this man is a murderer, whom, though he hath escaped the sea, yet vengeance suffereth not to live. **5** And he shook off the beast into the fire, and felt no harm. **6** Howbeit they looked when he should have swollen, or fallen down dead suddenly: but after they had looked a great while, and saw no harm come to him, they changed their minds, and said that he was a god.

2 Corinthians 11:23-26 (New Living Translation): 23 Are they servants of Christ? I know I sound like a madman, but I have served him far more! I have worked harder, been put in prison more often, been whipped times without number, and faced death again and again. **24** Five different times the Jewish leaders gave me thirty-nine lashes. **25** Three times I was beaten with rods. Once I was stoned. Three times I was shipwrecked. Once I spent a whole night and a day adrift at sea. **26** I have traveled on many long journeys. I have faced danger from rivers and from robbers. I have faced danger from my own people, the Jews, as well as from the Gentiles. I have faced danger in the cities, in the deserts, and on the seas. And I have faced danger from men who claim to be believers but are not.

Insurance companies make billions of dollars a year insuring peoples valuables. Homes, furniture, jewelry, watches, cars, boats, even body parts are insured. When a tragedy happens the person who bought the insurance contacts the insurance company and ideally they cash out on their policy quickly and move on.

The insurance concept also exists with God. Only thing is He is very interested and actually able to keep you alive. In other words as long as you are walking on Gods plan and purpose for yourself on Earth, you are immune to death. Even if you have several brushes with death or even die, God will bring you back over and over again. Gods plan and purpose in our lives is our insurance policy and nothing can kill you, however if you are not walking on your plan and purpose you are walking without an insurance policy.

You see, God has invested way too much into a person who on His mission. He has invested His Son, His Spirit, His heart, His love, His wisdom, His time, His angels, His finances and provision, His peace, His everything!! All this because He thinks your worth it.

Today, ask God what your plan and purpose is and if you haven't been walking under His insurance policy, sign up today! Your in good hands with... God.

~BRIDE~

Revelation 22:17 (Amplified Bible): 17 The [Holy] Spirit and the bride (the church, the true Christians) say, Come! And let him who is listening say, Come! And let everyone come who is thirsty [who is painfully conscious of his need of those things by which the soul is refreshed, supported, and strengthened]; and whoever [earnestly] desires to do it, let him come, take, appropriate, and drink the water of Life without cost.

There are many different Christian churches and different branches of Christianity, for example: Baptist, Evangelist, Catholic, etc. Although each branch may believe different things I am sure that each branch is trying to do the best they can. Some people believe that one has to be baptize at birth, whiles others believe that they have to be baptize at an age that they can recognize that they are sinners and need to be born again. Some do not believe in praying in tongues, while others believe that praying in tongues is communicating directly with God. Whatever you believe or whatever branch you pertain to there are some obvious red flags that let you know if your church is on fire or if your church is not on fire. Before we look at just 7 characteristics keep in mind there are more, but these seven are main ones. Also keep in mind that Jesus is coming for one bride not a bunch of them, as Christians we all need to unite and work together as one. When the Israelites took over Jericho they did so united not separated by their tribes. The enemy knows that by separating and causing discord between brothers and sisters through doctrine he has an advantage.

Lets pray first.... Father in the name of Jesus I pray that the Holy Spirit confronts each and every single person to ask themselves what kind of church are they in. Remind us all that church is not a social club but a place of worship. Father I pray that if Your children find themselves in a place that is not on fire, I ask that You send them and guide them to another place that is. In the name of Jesus. Amen.

Seven Characteristics:

1. The pastor or priest is sleeping in the morning and not seeking Gods face. They are passive and have no idea what God is doing, in other words they are not in the cutting edge of knowing what God is up to. They lack intimacy with God and do not fast, they pray without authority, and every service has the same schedule, this represents that they are not allowing the Holy Spirit room to conduct the service and they are constricting Him.

2. When the leaders of the church including the pastor or priest move in the flesh. Where there is sin of adultery, gossip, theft, manipulation, controlling, judgment, etc. That church is moving more in the flesh than in anything else and is constricting your spiritual growth.

3. When a women's calling is rejected or constricted.

4. Prayers are repetitive and religious. These types of prayers are based on 5 senses. Some pray for praises from others in order to please their ego, others pray without faith, and yet others just talk. Before one prays one must be aligned to Gods Will, His Words, they must pray in faith, authority, and believing.

5. Teachings are full of reasoning and intellectualism. Mostly theology is being taught. Reasoning will not change a person but Revelation will! Renew-Reform-Revelation! If the church is not talking about Gods supernatural power and glory, then where is the Holy Spirit? God talks to His people through His Words, one verse may be read one day and mean something completely different to you the next, depending on your circumstances and revelation.

6. Victory's without trails. If elders and mentors are being raised up in a democracy or voted in. Sorry, but Jesus didn't pick you because your perfect, He picked you and He knows He is going to have to work on you in order to make coal into a diamond. Example, some people say things like I will never leave this church, I am here till the end and someone gossips about them and they leave. Were is the growth, the maturity, the development of character to withstand. Someone gossips you stay and you continue your work, didn't they talk about Jesus? Guaranteed you go somewhere else your going to have the same problems so stay planted.

7. When they don't honor God. The music is the same, no prophetic songs; songs are songs of barely making it, instead of songs of victory and war. The worship is short or it just doesn't move you at all. The Word says that His habitat is in the middle of the adoration. No true adoration no presence.

Today, reflect and really ask yourself is my church flowing with the Holy Spirit or am I just making the enemies life easier by being part of a passive church with no authority.

~TIRE~

Matthew 26:41 (Amplified Bible): 41 All of you must keep awake (give strict attention, be cautious and active) and watch and pray, that you may not come into temptation. The spirit indeed is willing, but the flesh is weak.

Do not allow your faith to fall flat when you need it the most!

There are critical decisions that define who we are and what we stand for. During these moments guaranteed God is testing you and is allowing these circumstances to happen so you become aware of what is in your own heart.

Today reflect on Gods promises that He has given you personally and just know that although it may seem far away, trust that He is faithful. He knows that we are indeed willing but we are also flesh and fall short at times. Keep your faith going by praying and worshiping.

~Puppet?~

John 21:14-17 (Amplified Bible): 14 This was now the third time that Jesus revealed Himself (appeared, was manifest) to the disciples after He had risen from the dead. 15 When they had eaten, Jesus said to Simon Peter, Simon, son of John, do you love Me more than these [others do--with reasoning, intentional, spiritual devotion, as one loves the Father]? He said to Him, Yes, Lord, You know that I love You [that I have deep, instinctive, personal affection for You, as for a close friend]. He said to him, Feed My lambs. 16 Again He said to him the second time, Simon, son of John, do you love Me [with reasoning, intentional, spiritual devotion, as one loves the Father]? He said to Him, Yes, Lord, You know that I love You [that I have a deep, instinctive, personal affection for You, as for a close friend]. He said to him, Shepherd (tend) My sheep. 17 He said to him the third time, Simon, son of John, do you love Me [with a deep, instinctive, personal affection for Me, as for a close friend]? Peter was grieved (was saddened and hurt) that He should ask him the third time, Do you love Me? And he said to Him, Lord, You know everything; You know that I love You [that I have a deep, instinctive, personal affection for You, as for a close friend]. Jesus said to him, Feed My sheep.

If a neighbor asked you to feed their pet while they were away, would you? Many of us would with no problem. We would simply receive the instructions that included what to feed them, the times to feed them, the times to walk them, and a thank you. However if you neighbor said, please feed my pet forever, you may be more inclined to say no because that is now a more serious commitment.

The same things happen in Gods church, not everyone is meant to have that type of lifelong commitment to servings Gods people. In other words really about 10% of the church is called into full time ministry. This doesn't mean that we can't be part of amazing things or serve God in amazing ways.

Peter is obviously seen now in the Bible as a man of God, an Apostle, and someone who gave up everything to serve Jesus and he fed the flock, but if you think about that moment that Jesus asked him, 'do you love Me?' What must have been going on in Peter's head. Sometimes the same things happen to us, we rush through to get an answer without really thinking about it, and the same situation comes up, or the same question comes up and we rush through again to the same answer. When in reality the need to really contemplate what is being said is necessary, just as the need to commit and unite our words with our actions and our interior is imperative. It took Peter three times to really understand what Jesus was saying to him, but on the third shot it seems that Peter made that connection and was committed.

Today reflect on what you have been saying to others and take a moment to really see if your words reflect a united consensus in your being and ask yourself are you committed and up to what level, and if their is a level are you really committed? (There is no right or wrong answer so do not rush through your answer, simply reflect).

~Target~

Exodus 34:14 (King James Version): 14 For thou shalt worship no other god: for the LORD, whose name is Jealous, is a jealous God:

Psalm 78:58 (King James Version): 58 For they provoked him to anger with their high places, and moved him to jealousy with their graven images.

Exodus 2:3-5 (New Living Translation): 3 But when she could no longer hide him, she got a basket made of papyrus reeds and waterproofed it with tar and pitch. She put the baby in the basket and laid it among the reeds along the bank of the Nile River. 4 The baby's sister then stood at a distance, watching to see what would happen to him. 5 Soon Pharaoh's daughter came down to bathe in the river, and her attendants walked along the riverbank. When the princess saw the basket among the reeds, she sent her maid to get it for her.

Don't idolize things because they become targets!

Many times people do not associate God with feelings or emotions, and simply see Him as a God that loves everyone and anything, however this is not the case. Worshipping other gods or mixing ideas with the Word of God is something that really just sets God off. It is written in many verses in the Old Testament how the Israelites would go "whoring" after other gods and each time that would happen, God would become angry.

One time He had even decided to wipe out the Israelites, His own chosen people because of the things they were doing, and Moses spoke and pleaded with Him and convinced Him not to, and He didn't. Although God is merciful, slow to anger, and He loves us, He will not allow His children to put anything before Him because it's not good for us. You do not necessarily need to be worshiping other gods or bowing down to images, it may be that you put something in your heart before Him. Many things may take His place in your hearts alter: your job, money, your children, your spouse, your status, your own image of yourself, whatever it is ask Him to reveal it to you.

He may tolerate it for a while only because He is working with you, He may talk to you about it and perhaps send someone else to talk to you about it, however if you know that what your doing is wrong and you know He has spoken to you about it and it continues, be warned because what your idolizing becomes His number one target. In other words you just made God jealous.

Now lets not misinterpret nor jump to conclusions because this may sound selfish of Him, however it's quite the opposite. Its quite selfish of us, its by His mercy we are living and blessed, how is it that we don't put Him first and everything else second?

Now consider that you are idolizing over a person, maybe a child, spouse, mom, dad, a job, a business or whatever else and God has spoken to you about this, it doesn't necessarily mean that He will take that person or thing from you because He's a jealous and selfish. He may however move in ways to show you that that person or thing is not before him. For example if your child is the thing that is number one in your heart, in your strength you can't do very much to protect them, in fact common statements made by parents are that they have never felt so vulnerable until their baby was born. Now imagine giving that child to babysitter, still fell vulnerable? Of course you do, but imagine giving that baby to the best babysitter known to man, the babysitter that makes sure nothing will happen to your baby and can control everything, (even change peoples hearts) imagine giving that child to God, now whoever or whatever comes against that child comes against Him.

Still feel vulnerable? Would you take a dive in the Nile River? The same Nile River that has gargantuan crocodiles, Hippo's, and a slew of other dangerous and deadly animals. Well that's were baby Moses took a swim in as a three month old baby and not only did nothing happen to him, but he landed right in the hands of one of the most powerful people alive at that time, Pharaoh's daughter. So not only was he protected he was also blessed.

Do you see how this concept liberates you and sets you free? This applies for all areas. Once you have revelation about this topic and speak to Him about it He will comfort you, He will forgive you, He will bless you because know you are walking according to His statues.

We will never as long as we are in the flesh be able to understand God completely, (and most times its in retrospect that we finally get what He was doing with us) but the laws and statues He created for us are for our own good and open the doors for His amazing blessings.

Today if there is anything that you are putting before God ask Him for forgiveness and seek out intimacy with Him. We all have things that are hard for us to give up, but by giving them up to God and putting Him first there is freedom in knowing that we moved it from our limited hands to His unlimited hands.

~MANNA~

Exodus 16:19-20 (New Living Translation): 19 Then Moses told them, "Do not keep any of it until morning." **20** But some of them didn't listen and kept some of it until morning. But by then it was full of maggots and had a terrible smell. Moses was very angry with them.

Numbers 14:23-24 (New Living Translation): 23 They will never even see the land I swore to give their ancestors. None of those who have treated me with contempt will ever see it. **24** But my servant Caleb has a different attitude than the others have. He has remained loyal to me, so I will bring him into the land he explored. His descendants will possess their full share of that land.

Imagine being in the desert and seeing that the only food available to you came directly from God and was found on the ground on a daily basis. This alone is pretty confrontational, many believed at that time that food came from there own strengths and ability, however God has a way of putting things in perspective.

The Israelites were given direct orders from Moses dictating how much manna should be gathered, some of the Israelites disobeyed and attempted to gather more, and store it for later. Only to find out that the manna would spoil by morning with maggots and a stench.

God simply put the manna out there and through that He was able to show the Israelites their hearts. Greed, disobedience, gluttony, lack of faith, doubt that God could provide, complaints, arrogance, were just some of the things found in there hearts. How then could God bless a group of people that depended on their own understanding and reasoning? The answer is simple, He couldn't, so He just maintained them and their needs out of love and compassion. It was Gods desire to take them to better grounds were they all could be made prosperous and happy, but there own attitude didn't allow God to move.

The only ones that entered into the promise land from that generation were two men named Caleb and Joshua. These two men were sent to spy out the land with 10 others, and they were the only ones to believe that they could conquer the land through God; even though giants lived there. All the other spies were terrified at the grand statues of those giants and complained to Moses, and well in short they ended up dying outside the promise land. The next generation of the wondering Israelites also entered with Caleb and Joshua because they had a different perspective on things and God gave them the land right in there hands.

Today reflect on your attitude. Draw a line in your mind and choose your side, are you with Caleb and Joshua or are you with the group that wondered around the desert for a lifetime?

~Radical~

Deuteronomy 13:4-8 (New Living Translation): 4 Serve only the Lord your God and fear him alone. Obey his commands, listen to his voice, and cling to him. **5** The false prophets or visionaries who try to lead you astray must be put to death, for they encourage rebellion against the Lord your God, who redeemed you from slavery and brought you out of the land of Egypt. Since they try to lead you astray from the way the Lord your God commanded you to live, you must put them to death. In this way you will purge the evil from among you. **6** "Suppose someone secretly entices you—even your brother, your son or daughter, your beloved wife, or your closest friend—and says, 'Let us go worship other gods'—gods that neither you nor your ancestors have known. **7** They might suggest that you worship the gods of peoples who live nearby or who come from the ends of the earth. **8** But do not give in or listen. Have no pity, and do not spare or protect them.

GET RADICAL FOR GOD AND LET THIS STUFF GO!!!!

Please read: Psychic hotlines, Witch doctors, New Age, Scientology, Voodoo, Santeria, Horoscopes, Numerology, studying human aura, tarot card, palm reading, Chakras, Amethyst Amulets, Chakras Clairvoyance, Core Images, Crystals, Demonology, Energy Manipulation, Ghosts Haunting, I-Ching,

Learn Psychic Abilities, Learn Psychic Powers, Magic, Magick, Meditation, Wicca, Occult Books, Ouija board, Norse Runes, Paranormal Books, Paranormal Investigations, Poltergeist, Precognition Programming, black magic, white magic, Psiball Psionic Energies, Psionics, Psipunk, Psychic Abilities, Psychic Books, Psychic Potential Psychic Reading, Psychic Self-Defence, Psychic Sensitivity, Psychic Shields, brujerea, Psychic Vampirism, Psychokinesis, Psykers, ReikiRune Reading, Scanning Scepticism, Shamanism, Spirit Guide, mediums, Talismans, Tarot Telekinesis, Telepathy, dream catchers, hamsa bracelets, evil eye kabbalah jewelry, yoga, images of ying and yang, deep trans meditation, The Law of Attraction concepts, The Secret concepts, hypnosis, coffee readings, and having superstitious things or worshipping idols (including the Virgin Mary and Saints). **Now there is no excuse, no doubt, and no ignorance about what you should not be involved in.**

Many times we are invited by others to 'go check this out' only to be lured by an ignorant loved one into depending on others and their 'abilities' to show us the way. Sometimes our upbringing or culture makes us believe that these things are okay but there not. It's surprising how many Christians all over the world have one foot in with the enemy and don't even know it. Even things that appear harmless or knowledge-full that fall into these categories are not for you if you have been separated for God. In other words subscribing to astrological/horoscope readings on a social networks is in essence leading people astray. These things are also used by the enemy as stepping stones for other things, it all may start by a palm reading at a fair and end up in some spiritual consultant's office for advice. Do not open this spiritual door that makes you dependent on the enemy!

You want to know your future? Ask God, You want to save your marriage? Don't go to a "brujo" or in English a witch-doctor, or cast a spell, ask God to help you. You want protection? I guarantee you a bracelet wont save you neither on Earth nor in spirit. God saves, Jesus saves, protects, provides, unites, loves, Jesus restores, and He hears you with tender ears. You want to change your circumstances? Talk to God!

Today if you have ever dabbled or been involved in any of the things mentioned above or things not mentioned above, but you know your doing things that are not pleasing to Gods eyes, repent, ask God sincerely to forgive you, and then put those areas in His hands.

Prayer for you:

Father in the name of Jesus, Lord I pray for your children today, I pray God that Your merciful hand forgives each and every single one of us that have ever looked in the direction that Your Word prevents us from looking. In the name of Jesus and with Your mighty finger I break all binds and all pacts that Your children have made with the devil knowingly or unknowing. Father my soul constricts and begs for Your children, please remove the blinds from their eyes and correct them so they walk in Your path. In the name of Jesus I cut off the tongues of all those that whisper lies to Your children's ears. I cover each one of them with the Blood of Christ from the crown of their heads to the palm of their feet. I declare that you receive their apologies and put their sins in the bottom of the deepest sea. Give them all peace and show them, convince them especially those that doubt, convince them all that You are real, alive, and attentive, show them all that they can deposit their trust in You and be secure in knowing that You will fight their battles. Show them the awesomeness of Your unlimited power, grace, love, and set a fire in each one of their souls that ache for Your majestic presence. Father I pray in the Name above all names. Amen.

PART II: PRAYERS

Personal Note:

I highly encourage you to build a personal relationship, and these prayers should be used as guides. Fill in your own requests and petitions. The key to prayer is to pray according to Gods Will, which is found in the Bible. Starting a prayer should begin with some nice worship music, when you feel the presence of God then begin to pray for others. Ask the Holy Spirit to show you the people that need prayer then ask God to help you in the areas that you know He is working on you with. Finally pray about your petitions, when praying declare His Word over your petitions, for example, "Lord it is written that all things are possible to him that believeth, (Mark 9:23) and Lord I am believing You for a financial blessing (or whatever)."

~BEFORE PRAYING~

I declare in the name of Jesus that You God take control of the airs that Your glory and presence are here. I invite the Holy Spirit to this tabernacle and I worship You. In the name of Jesus, manifest Yourself Holy Spirit in a unique way today, I need You, I will not stop seeking Your face Lord until I feel Your presence. Father I unleash the power of the blood of Jesus over my life, over my children.

I bind all unclean spirits, and send them to lands of captivity declaring that they will not and cannot rise up against me or my future generations in the name of Jesus Christ of Nazareth. Amen.

~ADORATION~

John 4:24 (Amplified Bible): God is a Spirit (a spiritual Being) and those who worship Him must worship Him in spirit and in truth (reality).

Adoration

Father, I pray in the name of Jesus that You align my mind, body, and soul to worship You. I obligate that my flesh expels itself from all distractions, from all worries, from all natural thinking and that You manifest Your presence over me and all over Your children all over the world. I pray that You show me and each one of Your children how to worship You effectively. Lord give me revelation that worship is about You, and not something we do in our spare time but something we do as a priority. Give us hunger for Your presence; give us hunger for Your precious Word. Father show us how to humble ourselves in Your presence, show us how to receive everything we need from You in spirit and in truth. In the name of Jesus I declare that our adorations penetrate to the third heavens, that our adoration saturates the atmosphere. That we crown You with our songs and adoration. In the name of Jesus. Amen.

~PATERNITY~

Romans 8:15 (New Living Translation): So you have not received a spirit that makes you fearful slaves. Instead, you received God's Spirit when he adopted you as his own children. Now we call him, "Abba, Father."

Paternity

In Jesus name, Father I pray that You reveal Yourself to me as my Daddy. I pray that even if my own parents weren't the best, I know that Your love for me is so great that it surpasses human understanding, show me, Daddy, reveal it to me Daddy. Touch my heart, touch my mind, and change my interior Father. Lord give me revelation about what Paternity means to You in a church, raise up my pastors to be like You, with a heart like Yours and with eyes like Yours. Father I love You. Amen.

~Covered~

Psalm 91:11 (King James Version): For he shall give his angels charge over thee, to keep thee in all thy ways.

Covered

Father, in the name of Jesus, Lord I cover myself and my family with the Blood of Christ, I declare a hedge of protection over me and my family members (say the names out loud). I declare that no arm forged against me will prosper; I declare that all of the enemy's plans drop at my feet now. With the authority given to me as Your daughter/son, I bind all unclean spirits that have risen against me and my family and I order them to dry lands NOW! In the name of Jesus. Amen.

~TRUST~

2 Samuel 22:3 (King James Version): The God of my rock; in him will I trust: he is my shield, and the horn of my salvation, my high tower, and my refuge, my Savior; thou savest me from violence.

Trust

Father, in Jesus name I pray. Oh Holy Spirit guide my prayer, reveal to me the areas that I have a difficult time giving up. Show me the areas that impede me from getting closer to You Daddy. Father it is not always easy to comprehend why things happen, but I choose to trust You because You are my Rock, my Stronghold that will always hold me. Even though I may not understand everything at that moment, I know that You will reveal it to me at the right time and in a way that I can understand. Holy Spirit remind me and reveal to me that I have always been able to look back and see Your fidelity and Your Almighty hand at work. Show me that I can trust You, convince me that I can put all my being in Your merciful hands and I will be safe. In Jesus name. Amen.

~FORGIVEN~

Matthew 18:3 (Amplified Bible): And said, Truly I say to you, unless you repent (change, turn about) and become like little children [trusting, lowly, loving, forgiving], you can never enter the kingdom of heaven [at all].

Forgiven

Father... Abba! Oh God, please stop me from ever conforming to this world. Lord You sent Your son to die for my sins; He sacrificed Himself to save my loved ones and me. Give me revelation of His sacrifice, what it means, and how it sets me free. Lord I repent wholeheartedly for my sins and ask that the Holy Spirit confronts me before I sin again and I am able to stop. Break my heart down God and make my faith like a child's. Let me see Your Glory! In the name of Jesus I rebuke with all the authority given to me by my Father, all spirits of guilt, all spirits of depression, all spirits of anxiety, all spirits that whisper condemnation to my spirit, right now I put them all under my feet and declare that I am justified by the Blood of Jesus Christ. I was bought and made whole by my Lord and Savior and all my sins are nailed on the cross at Calvary. In the name of Jesus I renew my mind and declare that regardless of my sins I am forgiven and loved unconditionally by my Daddy. Thank You Jesus, thank You for setting me free from the bonds that my sins created. In Jesus name! Amen.

~Inheritance~

Acts 26:18 (King James Version): To open their eyes, and to turn them from darkness to light, and from the power of Satan unto God, that they may receive forgiveness of sins, and inheritance among them which are sanctified by faith that is in me.

Inheritance

Father, in the name of Jesus I give You praise and thanks. I declare my body a living sacrifice to be used to worship You with music and adorations, I declare my mouth to be a holy weapon that will bless Your children and launch attacks to the enemy that will obliterate him. I love what You love and abhor what You abhor. Thank You for forgiving me for all the times I have sinned in the past and how You keep forgiving me on a regular basis. Give me revelation of what I mean to You, show me what it means to be seated in celestial places next to Jesus, show me what having Your inheritance means. Show me the power that You have given me and how to use it. I humble myself and I submit to You Holy Spirit, mold me, and show me what it means to have Your DNA, Your authority. Show me, I am willing to learn and use it to serve Your children. In Jesus name. Amen.

~Revelation~

Acts 9:17-18 (Amplified Bible): So Ananias left and went into the house. And he laid his hands on Saul and said, Brother Saul, the Lord Jesus, Who appeared to you along the way by which you came here, has sent me that you may recover your sight and be filled with the Holy Spirit. And instantly something like scales fell from [Saul's] eyes, and he recovered his sight. Then he arose and was baptized,

Revelation

Father in the name of Jesus I pray that You consider the petitions of my heart. I pray that You give me revelation of Your Words, of Your presence, of Your plan and purpose for me on this Earth. Father I pray for revelation that will change my life, my life lens, I need to see things the way You see them, I need to understand things the way You understand them. Lord I pray that I do not stay at this spiritual level, I pray that You reveal to me what I need to do to advance Your Kingdom and how to help Your children. Lord reveal to me Father the power of prayer and intercession prayer, reveal to me Father the hidden treasures all around me both spiritually and financially. Reveal to me Lord Your spiritual laws that You established since the beginning of time. Daddy I am your daughter/son and I pray that You reveal to me Your love, in Jesus name. Amen.

~WORD~

Deuteronomy 8:3 (New Living Translation): Yes, he humbled you by letting you go hungry and then feeding you with manna, a food previously unknown to you and your ancestors. He did it to teach you that people do not live by bread alone; rather, we live by every word that comes from the mouth of the Lord.

Word

Father, Your Word says that man does not live by food alone, rather by the Words that You say, I pray that Your Words set me free. I pray that I have revelation of what Your Words mean. I declare in the name of Jesus that Your Words are the lamps at my feet that prevent me from falling into the enemy's traps. I declare that Your Words will confront me and change me taking me from glory to glory and from victory to victory. Lord I am only flesh and bones but I am still here and I am still hungry for Your life giving Promises. In Jesus name, Amen.

~Pact~

Hebrews 9:13-15 (New Living Translation: Under the old system, the blood of goats and bulls and the ashes of a young cow could cleanse people's bodies from ceremonial impurity. Just think how much more the blood of Christ will purify our consciences from sinful deeds so that we can worship the living God. For by the power of the eternal Spirit, Christ offered himself to God as a perfect sacrifice for our sins. That is why he is the one who mediates a new covenant between God and people, so that all who are called can receive the eternal inheritance God has promised them. For Christ died to set them free from the penalty of the sins they had committed under that first covenant.

Pact

Father, in the name of Jesus I come humbly before Your throne. I come as a daughter/son to ask that You cleanse me from all my sins and that You forgive me. I know I am justified and made right by Jesus Blood and when I mess up, His Blood rises up to defend me, to remind You of the new pact. Father I declare in the name of Jesus Lord and pray that You open the skies and let me see Your glory, Your great power in my life. I declare that what You have for me in heaven becomes established here on Earth, I declare that Your plan and purpose for my family and me are established in our lives in the name of Jesus. Amen.

~GENERATIONS~

Exodus 34:6-7 (Amplified Bible): And the Lord passed by before him, and proclaimed, The Lord! The Lord! A God merciful and gracious, slow to anger, and abundant in loving-kindness and truth, Keeping mercy and loving-kindness for thousands, forgiving iniquity and transgression and sin, but Who will by no means clear the guilty, visiting the iniquity of the fathers upon the children and the children's children, to the third and fourth generation.

Generations

Father in the name of Jesus, Lord I pray that You forgive my past generations for all their sins and all their inequities. I declare that by the Blood of Jesus Christ breaks all generational curses. I declare that no armed forged against me and my family will prosper. Lord I declare Your Word that says that if I direct my children onto the right path, when they are older, they will not leave it. I declare that You put a fire in them and a thirst for Your Words and ways. I declare that they grow up with one ear in the heavens and with one ear on Earth to hear Your voice. I declare that the seed You have implanted in their soul give fruit 100%. I declare that You are a God of generations and I cover myself and all my generations to come with the Blood of Christ. I order you

Satan to reverse your steps against them and declare that by the pact of Jesus Blood you have no authority and no part in their lives. I am reminding you that Jesus put you to shame at the Cross and everything yours was nailed their and crucified. I remind you that every drop of blood that fell from Jesus reminded you of how impotent you are and your end is in the lake of fire, you already lost and you are ordered illegal in my generations. I rebuke you and everything that is contrary to Gods Words. I bind you and I seal your mouth in Jesus name, that's right in Jesus name, the name above all names, and I send you to dry lands, to captive lands and declare that you cannot raise yourself against me or my future generations. In Jesus name. Amen.

~Unleash~

Matthew 16:19 (Amplified Bible): I will give you the keys of the kingdom of heaven; and whatever you bind (declare to be improper and unlawful) on earth must be what is already bound in heaven; and whatever you loose (declare lawful) on earth must be what is already loosed in heaven.

Unleash

In the name of Jesus, I come unleashing all that pertains to me; I come unleashing all the inheritance that my Father has for me in heaven and establish it here on Earth. I declare creative ideas are given to me, I declare hidden treasures are made known to me; I declare that all my blessings are established now. I loosen and establish holiness, peace, love, prosperity, and wisdom in abundance. I bind all unclean spirits that want to come against me, I bind all your plans against my family, my finances, my safety, and my health, I declare the enemies plan null and void. In the name of Jesus, Father I want to see Your glory, I want to see your power I want to see YOU! I love You Daddy. Amen.

~WAR~

Matthew 11:12 (Amplified Bible): And from the days of John the Baptist until the present time, the kingdom of heaven has endured violent assault, and violent men seize it by force [as a precious prize--a share in the heavenly kingdom is sought with most ardent zeal and intense exertion].

WAR

Lord, Your Words say that only the violent take by force the heavens. Lord today I unite myself to these Words and declare myself a warrior. I declare that I hear and recognize Your voice. I declare that I am that watchtower that watches over Your nation and Your children. I declare that I take my position in celestial places and will open my mouth to establish Your Kingdom here on Earth. I declare that my actions will be according to Your Will and I will submit myself to You. I declare myself positioned in the front lines committed to pray and intercede for those You put in my heart to do so. I declare that You reveal to me strategies to attack the enemy, and I pray that You expand my vocabulary so I can drop atomic bombs on the enemy's territories. I cover myself with the full of Your armor from Ephesians 6:13-17 (Amplified Bible): Therefore put on God's complete armor, that you may be able to resist and stand your ground on the evil day [of danger], and, having done all [the crisis demands], to stand [firmly in your place]. Stand therefore [hold your ground], having tightened the belt of truth around your loins and having put on the breastplate of integrity and of moral rectitude and right standing with God, And having shod your feet in preparation [to face the enemy with the firm-footed stability, the promptness, and the readiness produced by the good news] of the Gospel of peace. Lift up over all the [covering] shield of saving faith, upon which you can quench all the flaming missiles of the wicked [one]. And take the helmet of salvation and the sword that the Spirit wields, which is the Word of God.

~ENDING YOUR PRAYERS~

I cover my prayer with the Blood of Jesus, I declare that my beautiful heavily Father hears my supplication and prayers. I declare that any unclean spirit that comes against me, any spirits of vengeance, or any spirits of revenge that rise against me for this prayer, I order them now, right now in Jesus name, to be bound in chains and sent to captive lands. I cut off their tongues and declare them silent and order them illegal. In the name of Jesus. Father I pray that You send Your warrior angels from heaven to protect my loved ones and myself. Send them Daddy with their swords already unsheathed ready for the battle. In Jesus name I pray. Amen.

PART III: PSALMS

~Personal Note:~

Psalms are unique songs that come straight out of your soul. Psalms are like poems that create closer intimacy with God. They are utterly spiritually delicious to write and to read out loud to Him. David is known as a Psalmist of God, and God knew him as a man after His own heat. In David's most glorious hours and his darkest hours when his life was threatened, he always cried out to God. I encourage to you to entice God with songs of passion and desires of intimacy. These psalms are shared with you to give you an example, however God wants to hear your psalms.

~THANKSGIVING~

I shall raise my head up and put my eyes to the skies. I shall raise my arms up to the heavens. My heart will beat according to Your Will. My being shall be filled with Your presence. My lips shall declare loudly to all the nations You tell me to go, how much I love You. My face shall shine with Your glory because You live inside my being. I shall be forever thankful, forever shall I see You, and forever shall I feel You. Your loving hand caresses my head. Even if the land around me falls into desolate land, and I shall know that You are my God because I will have peace, and Your loving presence shall provide me comfort and joy. My eyes shalt not look at the circumstances; they shall be placed expectantly on You. Wind, storms, and hurricanes will not move me nor will man, materials, or money. They will not guide my steps, no, but Your steady voice and Words.

My feet feel the pulse of the living rock on which I stand and I know I shalt not fall nor wither away, oh God of my being I love You, I thank You, You are my Creator yet Your heart declares me Your daughter! Your beauty and love provoke me to passion and compassion. Thank You for breathing life in me not just when I came out of my mothers womb, but when I was empty and lost. Thank You for bringing feelings back to a heart once covered with armor and molts. Thank You for breaking me down to my essence with lassos of love only to have me rebuilt correctly, securely, and entirely.

Thank You for Your mighty love and desires for me, I can look back and see each time You called me by name and I ran away, yet You never forgot me. Without Your presence I pray that You take my life, without the certainty that Your with me, I would rather die and leave everything behind. Without You, then truly I have nothing but a mourningful soul. But I give thanks because You are with me and Your hand is extended out to me.

I feel You and Your presence makes my body shake, I recognize Your presence from before the foundations of the Earth were built, we were family, we were friends, we were in love and because of our past You died for me. I recognize Your sacrifice, I recognize Your voice, I know You, I know Your personality, I know You, and I thank You for knowing You. Thank You for bringing me back home and opening up my understanding and awakening my memory, I no longer have worldly amnesia, no, I have identity, I have a history with You and I have knowledge of what was, what is, and what will be through Your Words. Easy it is to say thank You, easy it is to say I need You, easy it is to say I worship You with all my being, easy it is to say You are my air, and even easier will it be to say I do when You come for Your church.

~CAPTIVATED~

Oh God where can I run, were can I hide from Your presence, were can I go that You won't find me? Can I climb the highest mountain to flee from You? Can I dive to the depths of the sea that Your hand will not signal me out? Can I run were You won't follow? Oh God, Lord, my Love, there is only but one escape I am interested in and that is to escape to Your arms. There I can rest and find a stronghold were nothing can touch me. Only there can I find safely for my heart, only there can I be free to express my love to You without words but in tears of joy. Finding You is like finding a hidden treasure so precious that one would sell everything to keep it. My treasure, my precious treasure. You have always been mine even from before I knew it. Finding You is like finding a Rose in a scorched land, like finding an oasis in midst of the desert. You are my river of living waters, You are the pulse that springs from my heart, You are my sweet Lilac fragrance in the summer airs, You are the breath that sustains my soul. You are everything I desire, there is nothing I need. In you I have everything.

~Beauty~

Is it a wonder why the angels sing to You? Is it a wonder why Your presence changed time? Is it a wonder why when people crash into You they are forever changed? Is it a wonder why You chose the least likely ones to be the most likely ones? Why are Your miracles a wonder? Why is a relationship with You a wonder? Why? Why are people so shocked? Why do some people doubt? Oh Lord Your majestic presence Father is so readily available for Your children, I pray that You open Your Kingdom up from in the heavens and show Your children Your glory. Jesus show them Your scars, oh God take the bands from their eyes and show them how much You desire them to be with You. Oh Father why is it so hard for them to see You?

~Consumed~

Oh my God, how You consume my thoughts, how You inspire me to be better. Lord You are the owner of my passion. You alone are the owner of my love. My flame yearns for You my God, my precious beauty.

Your eyes are as radiant as stars in the midnight skies, Your beauty is so intense I can't even control my stares. You are my hearts desire I love You more that any language invented by man could ever express. Feel the intensity of what You mean to me from the depths of my spirit, I thirst for You, I hunger for Your presence, I ache when I don't feel You around. Die will I if You leave me Lord. Your gentle caresses make the wiles of the world disappear, I hear nothing, I see nothing if its not You.

Jesus, Jesus, Jesus, amazing is Your name, beautiful is Your life my God, so loving, so caring, so wise. Today I give You my will, every beat of my heart is Yours, every breath I inhale is nothing compared to how much more I need You. With all my strength I will look for You, I will search You out and I will find You. Nothing can stop me from being close to You, and giving You my life.

~Exalted~

Lost and confused was I, materialist and guilty was I, selfish and irritable was I, scared and insecure was I, abused and abuser was I, broken and alone was I, tired and angry was I, arrogant and self serving was I, unsure and powerless was I, captive and in bonds was I.

Now, touched by You I am, stamped by Your Holy Spirit I am, separated and placed in heavenly places I am, blessed and covered by the power of Jesus Blood I am, fruitful and wise I am, faithful and strong I am, beautiful and imperfect I am, made from dust I am. Your breath is in me and secure and safe I am, frightful to the enemy I am. Daughter of the Most High God I am. Funny how I can say these things now, so different was I.

Graceful and forgiving are You, loving and concerned are You, Living and omnipresent are You, graceful and merciful are You, beautiful and confident are You, strong and secure are You, wise and funny are You, adventurous and playful are You, a great Provider and an amazing Teacher are You.

Oh my Lord thank You for investing in me when no one else would, You saw me but not the way I saw myself, You saw me how a prophet sees the end result. You have invested energy, time, angels, love, creative strategies, everything else it took to make me who I am today, so different, the old person is such a distant memory and I don't recall that girl. But I do see my life, and truly the Potters Hands have worked in my life, and continues to work in my life. Thank You God for Your love without You I would continue to be were I was, but because of You I am here at this moment. I love You and exalt Your name for the joy, peace, and love You have poured over me in abundance. I love You and I am happy with what You have done in my life.

~SALVATION PRAYER~

If you have never received Jesus as your Lord and Savior according to Romans 10:8-13 (New Living Translation): *(8 In fact, it says, "The message is very close at hand; it is on your lips and in your heart." And that message is the very message about faith that we preach: 9 If you confess with your mouth that Jesus is Lord and believe in your heart that God raised him from the dead, you will be saved. 10 For it is by believing in your heart that you are made right with God, and it is by confessing with your mouth that you are saved. 11 As the Scriptures tell us, "Anyone who trusts in him will never be disgraced."[b] 12 Jew and Gentile[c] are the same in this respect. They have the same Lord, who gives generously to all who call on him. 13 For "Everyone who calls on the name of the Lord will be saved.")*

Well, today is your day, breath in deeply and say with all your heart: "Father in heaven, I know that I am a sinner and have sinned. Please forgive me for my past sins, and I break all pacts with the devil and this world that I have made knowingly or unknowingly. In this moment I invite You Jesus into my heart and ask that You live with me everyday. Teach me and show me how to live. Holy Spirit I open my heart to You. I declare that Jesus is my Lord and Savior and I believe that He is the Son of God and He died for my sins. I know declare myself a child of the Most High God and declare that if I died at this very moment I would wake up in Jesus arms in heaven, in Jesus, Amen.

My Prayer For You:

In the name of Jesus, I cover the seed (which is the Word of God) with the blood of Christ and declare that it has landed in good soil. I pray that the seed sown in you gives fruit 100%. I declare in the name of Jesus that you reach your calling and find your purpose in Jesus. I declare that God will put a Holy fire in your soul that will make you hungry for His Word and hungry for intimacy with Him. In the name of Jesus I pray that everyday as you walk with Him that your eyes, ears, and heart is open to hear His voice and to see His awesome works. I declare that you will see Him work in your character, in your life, and in every other area in your life that needs His touch. In Jesus name. Amen.

About the Author

Rosie Soroka has worked in the mental health field for over ten years and has successfully ministered the Gospel of Jesus Christ both domestically and abroad to thousands of individuals, couples, teenagers, and children in all walks of life. She has worked with victims of domestic violence, family crisis, addictions, terminal illness, veterans, grieving families, incarcerated felons, and much more. She is someone who believes that all things are possible through Jesus, especially peace, healing, restoration, and love because she has experienced it first hand. The combination of her education in secular therapeutic techniques, and her powerful anointing combined have provided her a niche that few can rival. Throughout the years she has dedicated herself to intercession prayer, edifying hurting souls, exhorting Christians to find true intimacy with God and to unleash the Power of the Holy Spirit that lies inside each one of us. On a daily biases she imparts revelations on her blog site seen world wide at www.JCExpansion.com and offers Christian advice at www.Cornerofcomfort.com.